P9-BYT-141

William Langewiesche

Cutting for Sign

William Langewiesche is a correspondent for
The Atlantic Monthly. For many years a commercial
pilot, he now lives in California.

Cutting for Sign

William Langewiesche

VINTAGE DEPARTURES

Vintage Books

A Division of Random House, Inc.   New York

Thanks to William Whitworth, Cullen Murphy and the staff
of The Atlantic Monthly, where parts of this book have already appeared.

FIRST VINTAGE DEPARTURES EDITION, JUNE 1995

Copyright © 1993 by William Langewiesche

All rights reserved under International and Pan-American
Copyright Conventions. Published in the United States by Vintage Books,
a division of Random House, Inc., New York, and simultaneously in Canada
by Random House of Canada Limited, Toronto. Originally published in
hardcover by Pantheon Books, New York, in 1994.

Grateful acknowledgment is made to the following for permission to
reprint previously published material:

Funk & Wagnalls Corporation: Excerpt from *Druglord: The Life and Death of a
Mexican Kingpin* by Terrance E. Poppa. Copyright © 1990 by Terrance E.
Poppa. Reprinted by permission of Funk & Wagnalls Corporation.

Dr. Marianne Stockebrand: English translation of an excerpt
from *Architektur* by Donald Judd. Munster: Westfalischer Kunstverein,
1989. Marianne Stockebrand, Editor. Reprinted by permission.

The Library of Congress has cataloged the Pantheon edition as follows:
Langewiesche, William.
Cutting for sign/William Langewiesche.
p. cm.
ISBN 0-679-41113-5
1. Mexican-American Border Region. I. Title.
F787.L36 1994
972 .1—dc20   93-9040
CIP
Vintage ISBN: 0-679-75963-8

Book design by Maura Fadden-Rosenthal
Map design by Betty Duke

Photo courtesy of the author

Manufactured in the United States of America
10 9 8 7 6 5 4 3 2

To My Father

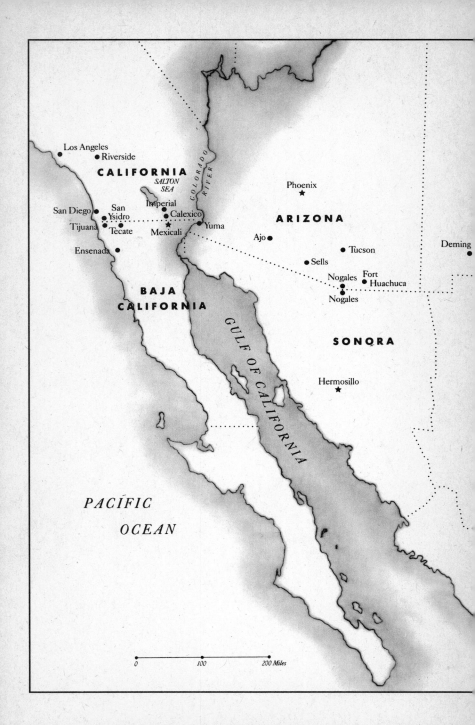

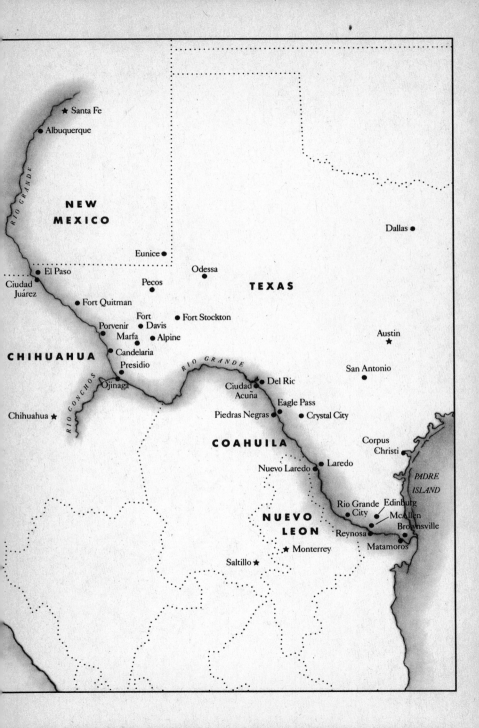

Cutting for Sign

One

I moved to Marfa to fly airplanes, and lived on a ranch about an hour's drive outside of town. Marfa lies in western Texas, in remote mountains by the Rio Grande border with Mexico. It is a land of sky, rock, and windblown grass. My first week on the ranch, an ornery old cow with a cancerous face grazed in the pasture below the house. She spent her days quietly in the shade of a mesquite tree, chewing slowly, covered with flies. One afternoon I watched her die, standing ground against a cowboy. He was a short, potbellied Mexican riding a broad-chested sorrel in the full strength of life. Together, they herded the old cow toward the shipping pen. Near the gate she rebelled. She stopped, turned, and bellowed. For a quarter hour she kept her antagonists at bay with the threat of her twisted horns. The cowboy cursed her viciously. It was a stalemate, or the mockery of one, until she lost patience and charged. The horse sidestepped easily and shouldered her to her knees. For the first time in her long life, she couldn't find the strength to rise again.

The desertion panicked her. She rocked on her knees and her bellowing grew high-pitched. The horse pranced in front of her. In the end she settled into the dirt with a groan and rolled onto her side, heaving. The flies settled onto her again. And the cowboy sat on the horse watching coldly. He stuck a pinch of tobacco under his lip and lifted a battered straw hat to let the wind cool his scalp. I thought he looked too satisfied: if this was a victory, it seemed a pointless one. He rode over to me, spat, and grinned. He had teeth the color of tobacco juice. His clothes were filthy. His face was fat, flat, copper-skinned.

In Spanish he said, "Dog food."

That was Ismael Zaragosa. We lived together on the ranch for more than a year, he in the crew cabin, I in the abandoned headquarters house, and out of necessity we became friends. I think he was nearly forty. He told me he was born in Candelaria, a hamlet on the Texas side of the Rio Grande. This made him a U.S. citizen, although he spoke hardly a word of English.

The ranch sprawled across twenty square miles of mountains and high grassy valleys. It was good pasture. Oaks lined the dry creeks and sparse pine forests grew on the ridge along the western perimeter. Once there had been year-round springs, but they had stopped flowing soon after the arrival of the cattlemen. Now, drinking water for the livestock was pumped by windmills from deep wells.

Ismael was the ranch plumber: every day he checked the holding tanks, pipelines, and troughs and made repairs. He spent the rest of his time riding fence, herding the half-wild cattle from one immense pasture to the next, and shoeing the horses. It was lonely work. In the spring and fall, big crews came in to help with the roundups. They called it shipping. The rancher lived in Marfa, and visited as seldom as possible. He gave Ismael his orders in profane border Spanish, every fifth word a form of *fuck*. He paid Ismael in cash and occasionally brought him groceries.

Ismael's needs were simple. He ate meat fried in animal fat, corn tortillas, and beans from the can. For entertainment, he had a few old photo-novellas, the subliterate melodramas of Latin America. He tuned his AM radio to a powerful station in Chihuahua, which broadcast *Norteño* ballads and personal messages to family members in the United States. The messages included more than happy birthdays and declarations of love: a mother was sick, a child was born, a man was urgently requested to come home. Ismael listened intently, though as far as I know he never received a message. Occasionally he got a telephone call from the store at Candelaria. The calls were mysterious. He didn't want me to know who was on the line.

The radio in Chihuahua ran advertisements extolling the virtues of Dr. Scholl's foot pads. This was during a time, before the immigration amnesty of 1986, when the mountains seethed with migrants walking north. It was odd how the ranchers, most of whom were patriots and racists, were willing to help. But the ethic of a wild land required it: no matter what your other prejudices, you had to respect the migrants for their strength and will. So the underground railroads ran all around Marfa. Our ranch was on a main line, and the Border Patrol knew it. Guards from the Marfa station came churning across our pastures in four-wheel-drive trucks, like overburdened hunters blundering through the woods. After they left, the migrants crept out of the creeks and canyons, and kept moving north. We never knew how many were out there, though over the years I saw hundreds. By the time they got to us they had walked three days from the Rio Grande across some of the harshest terrain in North America. They materialized at dusk and waited silently to be noticed. We gave them food and water, and let them sleep in the sheds. To those with bloody feet we gave soap and bandages. In the winter, when the ranch was blanketed by snow, they arrived frostbitten, with their heads wrapped in rags. We took them inside by a stove and gave them coffee. They had a hundred miles still to go. Mornings, they left as quietly as they had come, and were swallowed by the land.

The migrants were grateful, but not excessively so. Dignity was important to them, as it was to Ismael. He was polite to strangers, but kept his distance. They were on foot and he was not. It was a distinction which they all understood. This potbellied cowboy, who moved so awkwardly on his short legs, was transformed by the saddle. One morning he mounted before dawn and rode out across the pasture as the walkers were leaving, and I watched them watching. Few riders ever achieve such grace and mastery. His control was absolute. His lariat and rifle symbolized his power. The ranch was his fiefdom.

He did not attend church and I never saw him pray, but he had been infused with a Catholic morality. In some ways he was a prude. He did not often speak about women. Once at the ranch dump he pulled an old *Penthouse* from under a pile of rubbish and showed me the centerfold, a beautiful brunette in an Uncle Sam hat, saluting the stars and stripes. It was all Ismael could bear. He looked sideways at her, sucked in his breath, and burned his fingers on her chest. He said, "Hot!" and threw the image into the arroyo. I laughed, but he was half-serious. The rancher's son had brought the magazine from Marfa and disposed of it away from small-town eyes, and Ismael did not entirely approve.

I never saw him barechested, or for that matter bare-footed. He had two pairs of cowboy boots: heavy leather work boots, which he resoled with rubber cut from a tire, and pointed lizard-skin boots, which he never allowed to get dusty. He disapproved of drinking, but once a month would put on the fancy boots and ask me to drive him to town, to buy a case of beer. Back at the ranch, he would sit in his screened-in porch, turn on the radio, and start drinking.

He could drink most of that beer, stay conscious, and drink the rest. The drinking made him lonely, which made him drink more. After the first few beers, he began to croon and yelp with the songs on the radio. Drunker still, he slurred his words, staggered, and pissed in the yard. The danger period came later, when he sat on the porch firing his rifle through the screens. Because of this habit the screens were useless: flies flew in through the holes and trapped themselves in the empty beer cans, where they buzzed furiously. I knew to stay clear until the firing died down. Ismael entered the final stage when his eyes were bloodshot and glassy, and he could no longer speak. He looked then like a shaman on hallucinogens. And the radio played all night.

In the morning he would hobble around the stables, swearing off beer and saying, *"Cabron!* I'm hurt bad!" The pains penetrated deeper than a hangover. He felt them even when he had not been drinking; they hit him all over, seemingly at random, and sometimes laid him up for days. I helped him only once, when his face swelled and we figured a tooth had gone bad. I drove him to the dentist, a Christian who had killed a Mexican boy for climbing into his backyard to steal fruit. I read religious pamphlets in the waiting room while Ismael got his tooth pulled. It cost me only fifteen dollars. But the more serious pains remained. Over time I realized that no doctor would help, that somehow Ismael's whole world was what ailed him. A man can only stand so much. Ismael knew it too, and told me he did not expect to live to an old age.

He did not expect me to live long either, since he believed flying airplanes would inevitably get me killed. I was as alien to him as he was to me. He had no idea where I had come from. I tried to describe the man-made canyons of New York to him, but he had already heard about the Africans there and he needed to hear no more. I asked him if he had ever met a black man. He acted indignant at the question, and lied when he said yes. Once the conversation turned to Europe and I had to convince him that even if he persisted he would not find a way to ford the Atlantic. I showed him a world map and a postcard of the seacoast. But as a multiple of the Rio Grande the ocean remained an abstraction.

I must have seemed equally ignorant to him. We rode together and he tried to teach me about the ranch. He accepted that I did not know how to throw a rope or wrestle a calf to the ground. But he was mystified by my lack of exposure to death and my reluctance to kill. Ismael killed easily and often, and thought less of a man who did not. He wanted to help me with this. He demonstrated the remorseless cutting of a goat's throat despite its nearly human screams. He showed me the slaughter of chickens, rabbits, skunks, porcupines, bobcats, and coyotes, slaughter for slaughter's sake. To replenish our supply of venison, he taught me to hunt deer. I forced myself to shoot when there was a reason, but I never enjoyed the killing. Ismael did. When he crouched over dying animals I saw the same coldness, the same false victory that had showed on his face at the death of the cancerous cow. And I knew he would have killed people as readily.

The ranchers who met every morning at the Thunderbird restaurant warned me about Ismael's friendship. Surprised, I asked what they knew about him. They answered, nothing in particular. I was their pilot. They worried about me as you might about a nephew going native. But there was less chance of that than even I realized.

Ismael never spoke of family, and I assumed he was unmarried. Then one day Dora, his wife, caught a ride from the river and came to live on the ranch. Dora had crossed eyes and crippling headaches. She stood under five feet and was plump, dark, and very Indian. She came from Verrancos, one of the smuggling villages across the Rio Grande. I remember her sighs. The tragedy in her life was childlessness. She had a tiny dog named Ranchero, which she held against her chest and drummed gently as if he might need burping. Ismael never displayed his love for her, but he tried to please her. He did not drink in her presence. He listened patiently to her prayers. When her head ached, he made her lie down. When once she wanted fresh milk, he asked me to help herd a savage mother cow down the arroyo and into the pens. The mother cow was furious and aggressive, more dangerous than any bull. We got one rope around her neck, another around her thrashing rear legs, and risked our lives milking her. Dora made cheese.

Later I learned Dora was terrified of me, the first white man she had come close to. When Ismael rode out onto the ranch, leaving us alone, she hid in her house behind bolted doors. Nonetheless, when Ismael returned, she sometimes invited me to dinner. We ate outside in the dirt yard. One night I mentioned my amazement, still, that men had landed on the moon. Dora did not understand. She did not think of the moon as an object, or as something that could be walked on, but knew it simply as a light in the sky. Her lack of curiosity disoriented me. Afterward I never knew quite what to say to her.

Wild goats lived on the ranch. They were descendants of goats that had escaped from ranchers earlier in the century and bred in the mountains. Ismael wanted to capture them and build a herd for his retirement. He needed my help: the goats lived on the rocky summits of the highest ridges, and they were wary and nimble. Ismael's plan was to corner and rope them one by one. It took days of hard and dangerous riding, but over the months we were able to catch fifteen. Two we ate. The others milled about in a pen until Ismael arranged for a friend with a stock trailer to take them to the Rio Grande, where they were to lodge with Dora's family. The next afternoon someone phoned from Candelaria and reported that neither the friend nor the goats had appeared. Ismael swore immediately to kill his friend. I suggested he find the goats instead. I agreed to drive him to the river, but insisted he leave his rifle behind.

The night passed like a dream. We stopped at an adobe compound on the Rio Grande, heard a rumor, headed upstream on the U.S. side, went to a dance, left my car, got a ride across the river at the Candelaria ford with a man Ismael whispered was his enemy, and ended the chase past midnight with a shadowy group of men in a canyon twenty miles south of the border. No one had seen the goats. In frustration I insisted they could not have disappeared without a trace. Ismael answered that he already knew their fate: they had crossed the international bridge at Presidio, Texas, and been sold in Mexico. He shrugged and no longer seemed to care. This was odd. I should not have cared, but I did. I realized I hardly knew Ismael.

Two

I still return to Candelaria, Texas, which stands like a memory on the Rio Grande. It has an elementary school, an abandoned steam-driven cotton gin, a scattering of rough adobe houses, and the usual collection of junked cars. It also has a general store. Barren mountains, tinted blue by distance, climb the horizons. The river, which flows by silently between thickets of salt cedar, is about as wide and deep as a New England stream. The international boundary runs midchannel, but there are no fences and no border guards. Villagers from Mexico cross to the north on a suspended footbridge to buy groceries, to check their mail, and to visit friends. No one stops them unless they catch a ride and go too far, or try, after days of walking, to enter the modern world. Old Nellie Howard and her sister, Marian, tend the store. The two sisters owned the only well in Candelaria, all the land, and most of the houses. I asked Nellie why they had stayed. She answered, "Because we didn't notice the years going by."

It's true: when the sky turns pale with sunlight, and nothing moves, time seems to stand still. The heat rings in your ears. On a bluff above the store, ocotillos and prickly pear cacti grow among the ruins of a cavalry post. You can climb up there and look across the river into the village called San Antonio del Bravo, which lies just beyond shouting range. San Antonio is in the state of Chihuahua, in the desert of the same name. It is spare and dispersed, and would appear uninhabited except for the smoke drifting from a fire in a yard and a pickup truck creeping toward the river across abandoned fields. Farming is dead now and smuggling keeps the village alive.

Candelaria should be famous. From here, in 1919, the United States launched its last punitive expedition into Mexico. It was during the bloody Mexican Revolution, which embroiled the country in a decade of chaos. The expedition started with a job of bad navigation: two army pilots flying a DeHavilland biplane were patrolling upstream along the Rio Grande when they mistook a Mexican tributary called the Conchos for the main current. The Conchos flows in from the west, an unexpected orientation, and carries more water than the Rio Grande itself. Neither river looks important. From the air, the very idea of a boundary is diminished by the size and sameness of the view. Nonetheless the boundary is real, and by following the wrong river, the army pilots flew deep into trouble.

After an hour, they came to a railroad bridge that should not have existed. Some pilots would have blamed the map. These two understood their error and turned back. But then their engine quit. They crash-landed in the desert more than a hundred miles from the border. They tried to float down the Conchos River on a crude raft. The next day they were captured by Mexican bandits.

The bandits were led by Jesus "Pegleg" Renteria, who

had lost an arm and a leg while working on the railroad in Kansas. Apparently, the accident neither limited his mobility nor made him bitter: as he forced the captives through the mountains on horseback, he reminisced fondly with them about his life north of the border. He spoke good English. Encouraged, the pilots argued for their release. Renteria asked, "Do you want to die now?"

Several days later, the little group rode into San Antonio del Bravo, the village facing Candelaria. Renteria sent a message across the river to the U.S. Cavalry post: he would give up the pilots for fifteen thousand dollars. Otherwise, of course, he would kill them. The threat was real; the border has always given strength to men like Renteria, and allowed them to operate beyond any government's control. The message flashed upward through the chain of command. Washington protested to Mexico City, but quickly approved the ransom.

On the appointed night, the cavalry sent a captain named Matlack across the river with the first half of the payment. He made the exchange near San Antonio del Bravo, and returned safely to Candelaria with one pilot. On his next trip, he found the second pilot, with a Mexican guard, in a cornfield below the village. Matlack was not a timid man, and after displaying the remaining money, he yanked the pilot onto the saddle behind him, brandished a pistol, and forced the bandit to drop his rifle. According to a story that appeared several days later in the *San Antonio Express,* Matlack sent a message to Renteria to "go to hell." Renteria headed for the mountains instead. At dawn several columns of U.S. Cavalry forded the Rio Grande in pursuit.

Invading Mexico was a reflex of the time. Americans were tired of their chaotic southern neighbor. During the decade since the outbreak of revolution, civil strife in Mexico had killed nearly a million people—one of every fifteen Mexicans. And it had spilled too often across the boundary. The most famous incident occurred in 1916, when Pancho Villa sacked Columbus, New Mexico. In response, ten thousand U.S. troops rode into Chihuahua. Commanding them was General John Pershing, who had won acclaim suppressing insurgents in the Philippines. Chihuahua was not so easy. Moving lightly through the desert mountains, Villa hit and taunted the Americans, escaped them easily, and transformed himself from renegade into national hero. It was a brilliant and pertinent performance: since 1914, generations of Europeans had died in two years of frontal opposition, while here in the desert, the Mexicans showed the world how to dance with an enemy. The frustrated Americans withdrew in 1917, and, still tan from the Mexican sun, entered the war against the Germans in France. Once again, Pershing commanded. And along the border the Mexican raids continued.

Mexico's revolutionary Constitution of 1917 (which still governs the country today) declared that Mexican minerals shall belong to Mexico. This did not please the National Association for the Protection of American Rights in Mexico, a group of industrialists threatened by the nationalist drift of Mexican politics. Their worries proved justified: following the revolution, Mexico eventually did expropriate foreign-owned properties and retreat into protectionist economic policies. The industrialists wanted to forestall this with a military intervention. In 1919 they demanded either the annexation of northern Mexico or the establishment of a protectorate over the entire nation. Fresh from victory over Germany, the army also did some thinking on the matter. After mapping the terrain, it drew up contingency plans for an invasion of Mexico, including detailed lists of undesirables on both sides of the border who were to be arrested. Less confident minds prevailed, and the United States did not invade. But who could object to giving Jesus Renteria a short lesson in civics?

The Candelaria expedition echoed Pershing's earlier adventure. On the second day, the troops captured four men who had nothing to do with Renteria. The prisoners were turned over to the Texas Rangers, civilian lawmen who had tagged along for the ride. The Rangers had a reputation for roughness and a history of killing Mexican-Americans. They took the prisoners to the rear of the column and gunned them down. That night someone discovered two kegs of sotol, a fiery cactus liquor that laid out most of the soldiers until midmorning. On the third day, as they neared Renteria's hometown, Coyame, they heard that Mexican federal troops were approaching. Since the Americans were not authorized to start a war, they retreated and on the fifth day crossed back into the United States. The army claimed to have killed Renteria anyway, and gave an account of a gunfight between a biplane and a Mexican on horseback. Modern times. The next week, an Arizona newspaper got a letter from Renteria in which he mocked the story and made a claim of his own: while the soldiers had charged south, he had led his men north to El Paso to enjoy the ransom money. And why not? The boundary was easy to cross.

It still is. Despite all the efforts to enforce discipline on it, the boundary remains chaotic. As population and economic pressures have mounted, its permeability has become an essential feature of North American geography. Without an ocean, mountain range, or other natural barrier, the line is entirely a human construct—a legalism laid across the land. In the cities, it hardens into steel fences to keep immigrants out and does not work. In the open desert, it dwindles to three strands of barbed wire and works only to keep cattle from wandering. At Candelaria and along much of the Rio Grande, it is unmarked by any fence at all. This is not because powerful people intend to leave the border open. The boundary is too long and much too wild to police by normal means. Hiring more border guards has a larger effect in Washington, D.C., than here, where their patrols are largely symbolic. Building stronger gates simply encourages more people to walk around them. Sweeping the line with military radar is like shining a penlight through a dark forest.

Nonetheless, what is most surprising about the boundary is its power to divide. It has outlived the walls of Eastern Europe and has become perhaps the most potent political demarcation of our time. It cleaves the continent, separating rich from poor, strong from weak, north from south. Only here do the first and third worlds meet face-to-face, with no second world in between. The conflicts scar the open ground—and still the boundary holds. It can be crossed but never ignored.

From an airplane at low altitude, the line is easily visible. In the cities it looks like the divide between an orderly street grid and the confusion and smoke of a shantytown. In irrigated farmland it becomes the division between lush green acreage and narrow fields splotched with bare dirt. In cattle country it separates two pastures—one over-grazed and brushy, the other less so. Even at the confluence of the Conchos and the Rio Grande, where the army pilots got confused in 1919, the details now tell of division. On the Mexican side, a string of impoverished villages hugs the riverbank for seventy miles. They have adobe houses, adobe cantinas, cinder block churches, and maybe some Honda generators. The villages are connected by a rutted track that takes a full day to drive. The U.S. side is wilder and might seem abandoned. But the soil is torn where a Houston lawyer has dug an underground house. A mountainside is marked by the concrete prayer platforms of a New York art dealer, a mystic Muslim. And a paved road leads up the river all the way to Candelaria.

On the ground the divide is stronger still. When you cross the Rio Grande on the footbridge from Candelaria to San Antonio del Bravo, the air itself seems to change. It smells of dust and, closer to the village, of sewage. Children appear in abundance. The heat is oppressive and inescapable. A man in knit pants gives you water that tastes of salts and contaminants and seems to dry your mouth. You walk past the hut where a witch lives, past the government medical clinic and the elementary school, to the ruins of a chapel where plaster rubble litters the altar. In the store at the crossroad, a man wears a Japanese watch that plays "Dixie" on the hour. He wishes you away. The other residents are equally hostile: they think you have come to feast on their poverty or to inform on them. For safety, you need to cross back to the north before the sun goes down.

Crossing to the north has powerful effects. For the people of Candelaria, it has meant the chance to practice a slow absorption into the United States. Under immigration law, babies born in the United States can bootstrap their parents into the country. The boundary provides the definition to make this possible. By excluding Mexico, it protects people from their past. Even so, if you ask about the boundary, Candelarians will claim it hardly exists. They do not speak English, or watch American television, or read the newspapers. The United States still seems to them like a distant promise.

But a stranger can take the larger view. Candelaria lies closer to Dallas than to its neighbor across the Rio Grande. The babies will grow up and move on, and invite their parents with them. Candelaria will continue to be populated by newcomers, and San Antonio del Bravo by those who stay behind. The ideal of a shared humanity does not withstand the mapmaker's pen.

The boundary has a keeper. His name is Narendra Gunaji, and I spent a morning with him in El Paso, Texas, about 230 miles upriver from Candelaria. Gunaji is a trim, white-haired man with a severe disposition and the accent of his native India. He is an American success story—an immigrant with a Ph.D. and a ten-page résumé. For twenty-eight years he taught civil engineering at New Mexico State University in Las Cruces, where he also dabbled in Republican politics. In 1987 Ronald Reagan appointed him to head the U.S. section of the International Boundary and Water Commission. His Mexican counterpart, Arturo Herrera

Solis, is based across the Rio Grande, in Ciudad Juárez. Together the two men manage the physical boundary— the markers and waterflows along the 1,951 miles from the Pacific to the Gulf of Mexico. It is not a small task. Gunaji has 270 people working under him. When I got to the offices in El Paso, I heard a lot of "Yessir, Commissioner." Gunaji seemed to relish it. He gave the day's orders easily, with his arms folded. Then he took me for a ride along the boundary in the back of an official minivan, chauffeured by two assistants. One carried a cellular telephone.

The twin cities of El Paso and Juárez, with a combined population of two million, mark the midpoint of the border. This is where the Rio Grande, having flowed south from its origin in the Rockies, snakes through a gap in the desert mountains and turns southeast. It is also where the two halves of the boundary join: to the west the line runs crisply across the deserts; to the east it rides a more ambiguous midchannel course through the curves of the Rio Grande. For an engineer, these are two very different sorts of boundaries. The spot where they meet is a short drive from Gunaji's office, on the outskirts of the city. To get there, we crossed a rickety single-lane bridge and followed a gravel road along the Rio Grande. Boundary Monument No. 1 is an eleven-foot masonry obelisk in a postage-stamp park. There is no fence, since Mexicans crossing illegally into El Paso find the downtown more convenient. Gunaji encouraged me to stand with one foot in each country.

As an airplane flies, we were 645 miles from the Gulf of Mexico. Through innumerable meanders and one huge S-turn, the Rio Grande doubles that distance to 1,254 miles. Little of the water flowing by Monument No. 1 actually gets through; it is dammed and diverted for irrigation, and replaced by other waters that are dammed and diverted in turn. Nonetheless, you can imagine floating the eastern boundary in a boat. Allowing time to sleep and discounting delays in the two big reservoirs, it would take about a month. There are no dangerous rapids, but you would run the risks of sunburn, sewage, and occasional sniper fire.

At Monument No. 1 we were closer to the Pacific— only 585 air miles away. But even across dry land, the boundary follows an indirect route, totaling 698 miles. You could walk it in about a month, mostly through wilderness, without the slighest chance of getting lost. Gunaji's predecessors have erected several hundred obelisks of iron and masonry. The westernmost obelisk, Monument No. 258, is made of marble and is sometimes described as "historic" because it was the first one built, in 1849.

In El Paso the desert was growing hot. Gunaji wore a jacket and tie and sunglasses. He had begun to sweat and was tiring of my questions about dry land. The five-year surveys have become routine. The obelisks are like geologic features. The intermediate concrete posts are more vulnerable, but when one is knocked down, it simply gets replaced. What else is there to discuss? There is no glory in monuments. Gunaji wanted to move on to the Rio Grande.

I persisted. "What about graffiti?"

"Graffiti is everywhere. It's probably on the moon."

"It doesn't bother you?"

He smiled thinly. "I have a plan to keep the markers clean. I want to put up signs saying PLEASE PERFORM GRAFFITI AND PORNOGRAPHY HERE. AS GOOD AMERICANS."

Gunaji himself is a good American. He told me his story

after we climbed back into the air-conditioned van. He was raised in India in a family that was poor, lettered, and anti-British. His father, a lawyer active in the Indian National Congress, studied the American civil rights movement and wrote a book about Booker T. Washington. His older sister, jailed by the British and later called a freedom fighter, was married in a ceremony performed by Mahatma Gandhi. Young Gunaji was a patriot, but ambitious too. He graduated in engineering from the University of Poona, got a small job with the city of Bombay, and saved his rupees to buy a ticket out. There was no question where he would go.

El Paso is a strip city spreading along a freeway. Juárez is a slum. As the Rio Grande flows between them, it is hemmed in by twin levees, which are the domain of government. Gunaji had us driven downriver along the northern one, and sat with the pride of a proprietor in the back of the van. He was in an expansive mood. On the opposite shore the tin and scrapwood shantytowns sprawled over low hills. The Juárez slums are as bad as others along the border. They are as bad as the slums of Bombay. I wondered if they reminded Gunaji of his past. A gully spewed black water into the river. Tainted upstream by agricultural runoff, the Rio Grande swallowed the filth easily. A family bathed among the bushes. The men had stripped down to their shorts; out of modesty the women had kept their dresses on. They stood in the water and watched us pass, a world away. Ahead, the bridges between Juárez and El Paso spanned the river. A rowboat heavy with passengers nosed against the U.S. shore, bypassing immigration formalities. One woman couldn't climb the steep embankment. Others, who had already made it to the top, went back down to help.

The young Gunaji had no one to help him. He got a student visa, came to New York by ship, took a train to Madison, Wisconsin, and started graduate studies on his last twelve dollars. He worked as a dishwasher and soda jerk, lived upstairs, got a scholarship and eventually a doctorate, fell in love with an American, married her, had five children, became a professor and ultimately a consultant. He said without irony, "I stand as an example that the American dream is still alive."

Other examples stood outside. Sealed in the van, we crept through a crowd on the levee. Perhaps a hundred people waited there, getting their bearings and watching for the Border Patrol. Though the levee is technically U.S. territory, in practice it is neutral soil, since retreat to the river is easy. The crowd was mostly local—unemployed Juárez youths without border-crossing cards going to El Paso for the day. A few, however, were greater travelers. They had come from the interior of Mexico, or from Central or South America, and they were going farther than El Paso. They carried suitcases and scurried away from the van. The locals were not so shy. Recognizing the boundary commission seal on the door, they tapped on the roof, peered through the windows, smirked, and joked. They begged cigarettes, which we did not have. Boys stood in the van's way nonchalantly, showing off for girls. Gunaji's assistants exchanged long-suffering looks.

Gunaji seemed oblivious. He spoke about his decision to become an American citizen. His older sister objected, but he had prepared an argument for her. "I told her, 'I'm going to serve India by staying out of India.' "

I interrupted him. "Doesn't it seem odd, if you think back, to find yourself managing this boundary?" I gestured toward the crowd.

He looked annoyed. "In the United States I have always tried to participate in the workings of government. I served on the Las Cruces City Council. Now I serve as commissioner. I am happy such an honor has been bestowed upon my family. A nation needs its boundaries, no?"

I nodded yes. You need a *them* to have an *us*.

We drove downriver to the Free Bridge, so called because no tolls are charged. The Free Bridge belongs to the boundary commission. It spans the Rio Grande at a patch of riverland named the Chamizal, after the desert grass *chamizo* that once grew there. The Chamizal is Mexican territory that was lopped off and delivered to the United States in 1864 by a southward shift of the river. This event kicked off a century of squabbling. The remedy, finally agreed upon in 1963, was radical surgery: 4.3 miles of new concrete riverbed were laid and the Free Bridge was built. On December 13, 1968, Lyndon Johnson came to town, met Mexican President Díaz Ordaz at the border, and diverted the Rio Grande into its new course. Mexico walked away with a net gain of 437.18 acres. On the U.S. side, Johnson has still not been forgiven. The problem is, one nation's gain is another's loss. And the boundary commission is guilty by association.

I learned this within minutes of landing at the El Paso airport, having mentioned to a pilot that I had come to visit the commission. "Those sons-a-bitches," he said. "They're the ones who gave away Texas."

24

He assumed I shared his sentiment, since I, too, had lived in Texas and had flown the border as an air-taxi pilot. He was less open-minded about Gunaji, whom he had seen on television. He said, "Who the hell is that guy? I can't even understand when he speaks English."

It was not a good week for Gunaji. We stood in the shade of the Free Bridge and watched workmen drilling into the concrete. The bridge was rotting. It was built by the Mexicans, of substandard materials, long before Gunaji's time, but it was his problem now. He had ordered emergency shoring. Yesterday he had banned the truckers who haul cargo to and from the *maquiladoras,* the big American assembly plants in Juárez. Hundreds of these drivers make short runs across the border with Mexican rigs loaded to 100,000 pounds. The Free Bridge is their cheapest and most convenient route. Gunaji had forced them twenty miles downriver to the toll bridge at Zaragosa. People were outraged because, after all, the Free Bridge had not yet collapsed. The American managers of the *maquiladoras* threatened to go to Washington over Gunaji's head. There was talk of conspiracy and corruption. There was talk of violence. Now Gunaji stood under the bridge with his arms folded, looking alone and defiant. Watching him, I thought I understood the severity of his mood. He was an engineer trying to do his job. Other boundary engineers have certainly been allowed to do theirs.

The remaking of the Rio Grande at the Chamizal was not the first operation of its kind. In the 1930s the boundary commission rectified the river downstream from El Paso. Rectified means this: the meanders were cut off, the river was straightened and run between levees, and the length of the boundary from El Paso to Fort Quitman was shortened from 155 to 86 miles. The two countries exchanged 6,920 acres of land in equal amounts, and none of Texas was lost. Here and there the commission has rectified the Rio Grande all the way to the Gulf of Mexico.

But rivers make old-fashioned, troublesome boundaries. One problem lies beyond Fort Quitman, where the rectification ends and the Rio Grande resumes its natural course between faulted mountains. For 198 miles downriver, past Candelaria to the confluence of the Conchos, the Rio Grande braids through jungles of salt cedar. Salt cedar is not a native plant. It is a bush or small tree, a tamarisk brought to North America from the Mediterranean in 1852, sold in California as an ornamental, and planted in New Mexico to control erosion. By the end of the century it had infested riverbanks through the desert and beyond. It is estimated now that 1.5 million acres of salt cedar grow in the American west. The seeds drift in the wind and when they land on moist sand, they plunge taproots thirty feet deep into the permanent water that lies below riverbeds. The taproots make salt cedar resistant to drought and flood, the on-again, off-again condition of desert rivers, and allow the plant to dominate the less robust native species. The domination is not all bad: salt cedar provide an ideal habitat for birds and other creatures. However, by clogging established channels, it also forces floodwaters to spread farther and encourages rivers to braid. Braiding is the untidy process by which a current laden with sand and silt restlessly builds bars, then divides around them. It is a particular problem on the Rio Grande because it makes the location of the channel, and therefore of the boundary, impossible to establish. The imprecision bothers surveyors, if not the residents.

In the 1970s the commission decided on an engineering solution: for these 198 miles the river would be made to follow the boundary. The two countries agreed. The commission filed environmental-impact statements, compromised with conservationists, promised to "enhance wildlife," and in 1980 unleashed the bulldozers. The work continues today, shared by the two countries. The channel is being "restored" to an angled cross-section six feet deep, sixteen feet wide at the bottom, and thirty-eight feet wide at the top. A V-shape is the most efficient design because it minimizes evaporation and encourages the scouring action of a fast, smooth flow. Floodways fifty-six feet wide are being scraped through the salt cedar along both banks.

Nellie Howard, the old sister in the Candelaria store, was not impressed. She said, "When they channelized the Rio Grande, they forgot it was a river and tried to give us a ditch. Come the first rain, the water went everywhere." Soon after work was completed in Candelaria, thunderstorms burst on the mountains and filled the creek beds with torrents for two days. The Rio Grande went wild and returned nearly to its natural state. Nellie Howard smiled and said, "Those engineers came down here pretending to know everything. We tried to tell them, but they wouldn't listen. The river reminded them who's really in charge."

Gunaji himself must wonder. One warm spring day I accompanied him on a working tour of the banks downriver from Candelaria. Our guide was the boundary commission's local engineer, a burly man named John. He drove us in a Ford Bronco along a recently repaired dike, past fields of blue wildflowers. Gunaji was in another of his expansive moods and sat with his arm over the seat back. He said, "What are these flowers, John?"

"Weeds, Commissioner."

"They may be weeds, John, but they bring color to the country, John."

"Yessir, Commissioner."

Later Gunaji seemed to remember his mission. He turned to me with a frown and said, "You see all this vegetation? We need to mitigate this vegetation."

I asked why.

He said, "It impedes the water."

And the water impedes the boundary commission. The project is years behind schedule. There have been difficulties with earth-moving equipment and international coordination. Floods have washed away the floodways. And salt cedar, which can grow nine feet a year, spreads as fast as it can be cleared. From the air the river looks like it has always looked. The conservationists must be pleased. They agreed to a compromise, but this is better because the river itself is fighting back.

The engineers, however, show no signs of fatigue. They are armed with a 1970 treaty that resolved all pending boundary disputes, reaffirmed the channel as the dividing line, and forbade any further misbehavior by the water. The Rio Grande has become boundary first and river second. And time is on the side of government.

The U.S.-Mexico border is, of course, wider and more intricate than a simple boundary line. Defining it is a problem that concerns members of a group called the Association of Borderland Scholars. Traditionalists among them concentrate on the fifteen sets of twin cities and the seven million people who straddle the line. More muscular scholars feel less constrained. They refer to a "zone of influence" perhaps sixty miles wide on either side. With one simple assertion they double their population base. And why not? If they stretch a bit more, they can include Tucson, which is a pleasant city to study.

Global thinkers stretch even further. In Mexico they point to the explosive growth of the north, the recent U.S.-inspired economic reforms, and the corruption unleashed by drug smuggling. In the United States they point to immigration problems, industrial decay, and unlawfulness. They say the border is everywhere. And they have a point: you can separate the two nations, but you cannot know one without the other.

The border is a word game.

It is also grimy, hot, and hostile. In most places it is ugly. The food is bad, the prices are high, and there are no good bookstores. The U.S. side is depressed by the filth and poverty in Mexico. The Mexican side is overrun by destitute peasants and roiled by American values. The border is transient. The border is dangerous. The border is crass. It is not the place to visit on your next vacation.

Neither the United States nor Mexico wanted this intimacy. The boundary was drawn after a two-year war of conquest, during which U.S. troops invaded northern Mexico and occupied Mexico City. By the terms of the Treaty of Guadalupe Hidalgo (1848) and the subsequent Gadsden Purchase (1853), Mexico was forced to cede the northern two-fifths of its territory, a national tragedy it has not forgotten. The role of U.S. business in the human exploitation that eventually led to the Mexican Revolution added to the resentment. For these reasons and others, anti-Americanism has long been a strong element of the Mexican national character. It has mellowed, but only recently, and—despite the new political rhetoric—unsurely.

The United States has less complex emotions: it would have preferred a second Canada on its southern flank. The current move toward economic integration, which consists largely of reducing trade barriers, is an attempt to create just that. It is also the recognition of an uncomfortable reality, that the border is no longer remote and can no longer serve as a buffer against the troubled south. Quite the opposite: on both sides, the border's explosive growth has physically bound the two countries, and Mexico's problems have inevitably become ours.

In Mexico the sense of urgency is infinitely stronger. Free trade with the United States is only one element in an attempt to rework the very basis of national life. It is by now a familiar story: protectionist economic policies and domestic populism have been scrapped in favor of unfettered free market capitalism. Such changes do not come easily, but Mexico was terrified into action. Diplomatic niceties do not make this clear: the nation is sick with debt, cynicism, and inefficiency. Mexicans use the word *cancer,* and say it has metastasized. The carcinogen was oil. Mexico sits on some of the largest reserves in the world. The rise in oil prices of the 1970s—what we in the north called the energy crisis—meant that Mexico suddenly looked rich. Flush with petrodollars from the Middle East, banks in the United States and Europe rushed to Mexico to lend money. Mexico gladly accepted their offers. Counting on a future of big oil revenues, it overborrowed and overspent. Then when oil prices dropped, the petrodollars evaporated and the structure collapsed. In August 1982, Mexico threatened to default.

The Reagan administration answered with a multi-billion-dollar emergency package. Eventually the loans were rescheduled—a solution that allowed the bankers to keep showing the questionable debt as an asset. But the banks were not eager to lend more. The peso collapsed, inflation ran wild, and the Mexican economy spiraled out of control.

After airplane accidents, investigators sometimes write about "negative climb rates" before the impact. By this they mean the airplane should have climbed, and didn't. Economists writing about Mexico use a similar term— "negative growth"—to describe the 1980s. They mean the rich didn't get richer and the poor kept getting poorer. Most Mexicans are poor and most are young. The country's current birthrate of 2.2 percent, though lower than past rates, means that the population of 84 million will grow to 100 million by the year 2000. The question is not only will the economy keep up, but will it satisfy? Someone may already have described the problem as a negative decline in human expectation.

All this bears on another word, *revolution*, which on the banners of the ruling Institutional Revolutionary Party (PRI) refers only to the glorious past, not to intentions for the future. *Counterrevolution* is the best description of Mexico's present policies. They amount to competition, entrepreneurship, and investment from abroad, the American way. Acting by decree, the government has slashed import duties, privatized banks and national industries, and re-written the laws that once excluded foreign companies. "Foreign" in Mexico usually means "Yankee," and the invitation to investors has renewed old questions of national sovereignty. But Mexico sees little choice.

By external measures, there has been progress. Inflation has dropped from 200 to 20 percent, interest rates have fallen, the proceeds from the sale of the public companies have been used to reduce the national debt, and much of the Mexican capital that fled overseas has returned. The Mexican economy is said to be growing by over 3 percent a year, and Mexico is now held up to other Latin American countries by the United States as an example of good behavior. But the improvement has not come fast enough. Despite Mexico's sincerity and its promise of cheap labor, foreign investors still worry about corruption, political instability, and poor infrastructure. Everyone remembers that external measures of progress proceeded the last revolution.

In the early 1990s Mexico's government concluded that the pot needed further sweetening—for instance, a promise to those investing in Mexico that they would have unfettered access to the greatest consumer market on earth. A free trade agreement came to mind because the United States and Canada had signed one in 1989. When Mexico approached the United States for a deal, it found a willing audience.

Nonetheless, there was opposition—labor unionists, who worried about low wages and the loss of factory jobs, and environmentalists, who worried about unchecked industrial pollution, did not necessarily want to encourage

Mexico's growth. The Canadians had their own questions about fairness, based to some extent on their experience with the earlier free trade agreement. The Mexican stock market reflected American and Canadian doubts even before the electoral victory of William Clinton sent prices diving.

The free trade debate unleashed a frenzy of conferences and policy papers at universities and policy institutes. For Mexico specialists, long consigned to the dim corners of academia, the day of glory had finally arrived. Though some took the side of the critics, most seemed to approve of free trade and agreed that Mexico's economic reforms were long overdue. I was surprised by their certainties. In the wood-paneled office of one historian I said, "But don't the Mexicans have a reason, historically, to fear us?"

He pouted and fluttered his hand. "That's the old divisive way of thinking. Learn to think ahead!"

So I asked, "Do you think it's smart to assume political responsibility for Mexico's gamble?"

He answered, "Can the United States allow Mexico to fail?"

His question raised the ghosts of past interventions in other places. There is usually some reason to fear change. It is true, however, that for the United States Mexico is not just another country. The two nations are now joined like Siamese twins, and are incomplete, one without the other. So the professor had a point.

Three

It was morning in San Ysidro, California, and the air blew cool with an ocean breeze. San Ysidro is the southernmost district of San Diego, where the city presses hard against Tijuana, Mexico. I stood at the border fence while a band of boys came over the top. The fence is a ten-foot steel wall and it supported their weight easily. The boys wore jeans, T-shirts, and sneakers and carried no luggage. The last one balanced on top and watched his friends dashing north toward a Kmart. He was thin, red-haired, and clearly disgusted by their haste. I guessed he was twelve or thirteen. He glanced at me, seeking eye contact, wanting me to know he was unafraid. To prove it, he turned and dropped through a full back flip into the United States. He landed beside me with a thump and a grunt. In Spanish I said, "What's happening?" He answered, "Not much," and ambled off into the city.

Not everyone is athletic enough to go over the top. At night, enterprising Mexicans dig holes underneath the fence and charge a dollar for each passage. They also hack right through the steel. I watched a matronly woman squeeze through one gap. She had to bend and step sideways to protect her dress, and she seemed annoyed that the gap had not been made wider. Once on U.S. soil, she dusted off her clothes, gave me a quick glance, and wobbled down the gravel embankment on high heels.

This so-called war zone, where illegal immigration is at its most brazen and where enforcement is concentrated, runs from the Pacific Ocean through brushland and city streets to the first desert mountains, a distance of only fourteen miles. The official crossing point, the port of entry, is a dryland gate in an urban sprawl. It is in fact two gates—one Mexican and one American—big, boastful structures spanning a north-south freeway. Together they tally fifty million crossings a year and claim to be the busiest border point in the world. Southbound traffic slows but rarely stops. Northbound traffic backs up for miles and crawls through a multilane marketplace that has grown up around it. Day after day in the fumes, boys wash windows, girls sell gum, and Indian mothers beg for charity. From the comfort of your car, you can buy what you need: genuine peasant clothes, cartoon dolls, Maria and Jesus, a giant beer mug, a plastic dog or cactus, an etched mirror, a pelican on a piling, and even death itself—a grinning skeleton in an infantry helmet riding wide open on a dirt bike. The waiting can last hours. At the end a green light says come, one car at a time, and a gatekeeper says stop, now prove your right to proceed.

Millions of Mexicans do not have that right and cannot get it. If they followed the rules, they would wait a lifetime at the port of entry. So they cross illegally. Those with good counterfeit documents pass brazenly through the port. Those with bad counterfeits—about fifty thousand annually—get turned back. Many more simply sidestep the formalities and hit the fence. They do not do this secretly: watching them come is one of the more interesting sights of our time. During the day, they trickle across. At night, they come through the darkness in waves. They succeed by the weight of their numbers. The Immigration Reform and Control Act of 1986 was meant to solve the problem. The gatekeepers cling forlornly to it. "The law should have worked," they say. But the immigrants feel neither reformed nor controlled. California still beckons.

Officials estimate that half of all immigrants illegally entering the United States cross the border here. The immigrants choose San Diego not just because the crossing is easy (it is easy everywhere except across the harshest deserts), but because it is rewarding. Even during hard times, California hustles relentlessly. The hustle starts in Tijuana, where ambitious workers arrive by bus from throughout Mexico and Central America. A city of more than one million inhabitants, Tijuana has developed the kind of economy that free trade proponents promise for all of Mexico—industrial growth, full employment, and factories that pay workers seven dollars a day. It is no wonder that many of the new arrivals keep going. They are met at the bus station by *"coyotes,"* smugglers who lead them across the border and lose them in the California crowds. In California they can find friends and family, and jobs that pay five dollars an hour.

Every morning for a few hours the border lies exhausted. Hard-packed and scarred by polished trails, the ground is littered with candy wrappers and discarded clothes. From the port of entry you can walk along the fence to the place where the Tijuana River flows in from Mexico. The Tijuana River is an open sewer. After it enters the United States, it turns west and runs between massive levees, parallel to the boundary. An indignant San Diegan instructed me to "go look how the Mexicans pointed that river at us!" But the river was once a natural flow and it still approximates its original short course to the ocean.

I found a bulldozer clearing bushes from the banks. Bushes make good cover, especially at night. Some congressmen claim that by "sanitizing" the border, by razing the vegetation and installing powerful lights, the United States can reduce illegal immigration. But I saw a family cross in bright sunlight within a hundred feet of the bulldozer. The father led, followed by four children and the mother. They balanced on tires that had been laid across the shallow river like stepping-stones. After they left, the bulldozer eased into the current and pushed the tires onto the south bank. I thought the tires should have been piled on the north side. The man on the bulldozer probably knew it made no difference.

Later a young man shepherded a group of Indian women across. Wearing plastic bags around their legs, they bunched together and waded shin-deep through the filthy water. On dry ground again, they stooped and peeled off the leg protectors. The bank was littered with hundreds of these bags; vendors sell them on the south side for a dollar a pair, rubber bands included. The guide told the women to wait, and he scrambled up the levee to scout for the Border Patrol. He stood near me, breathing heavily, checking the neighborhood. We did not speak. He beckoned to his group and they started up, bent forward against the slope. Suddenly a green Border Patrol Bronco drove onto the levee and accelerated toward us. The women retreated to the river. The guide took two steps down the levee and stood his ground. The border guard stopped above him and didn't bother to get out. He was a burly man in a green uniform and a felt cowboy hat. My presence bothered him. Except for a Quaker "peace patrol," which watches for Border Patrol excesses, there are few Anglo visitors. The guard backed away and parked below the levee in a field. He seemed confused. The guide returned and squatted comfortably. He seemed amused.

That afternoon I followed the Tijuana River downstream to the ocean through an eerie valley given over to the war. There are killings, rapes, and robberies. The river is diseased and the stench of sewage is inescapable. Placards with skulls and crossbones warn of contamination. Coastal winds stir clouds of fine-grained fecal dust, making you want to cover your face when you breathe. There is a park called Border Field, which no one visits, where Boundary Monument No. 258 stands in unadmired marble splendor. There is a sod farm, a nursery, and a stable that advertises horse rentals, though it's hard to imagine anyone would go for a ride. There is a house enclosed by a stout fence and guarded by aggressive dogs. Down the road, a hand-painted sign reads NO MAN'S LAND.

The boundary runs just to the south along the crest of low hills. All day the crowds gather in increasing numbers at the fence. By late afternoon you see hundreds up there, dark lines of people waiting for the sun to set. Vendors sell drinks and tacos. Where the fence is torn, the immigrants swell through and stand inside the United States. Border guards square off against them in scattered trucks, radios crackling. They face a near riot, an afternoon ritual. The fence marks the territory they intend to defend, but they keep a wary distance from it: it serves the unintended purpose of sheltering the Tijuana toughs who jeer and throw rocks. The irony is not lost on the guards.

At dusk the line crumbles. The movement starts slowly, here and there, as the most eager travelers leave the safety of the fence. Their success encourages others, who follow in increasing numbers. Seen from the valley, the immigrants look like dark specks streaming over the hillsides. The first group crosses Monument Road, close to where you stand. Men and women emerge from a gulch in single file and melt into the gloom. You wonder in the twilight if your mind has tricked you, but then you see another group, and another. Up at the fence, the flow accelerates and with the oncoming night becomes relentless. The Border Patrol fights back, driving furiously, and is overwhelmed. The valley turns black under ocean clouds, and fills with immigrants moving north. Banks of portable floodlights switch on, casting harsh beams on insects and dust, plunging the rest of the night deeper into darkness. A dog barks viciously. Two border guards materialize, riding darkened all-terrain quad-runners. With their uniforms and full helmets they look like the soldiers of a nightmare future. They herd a man in sandals and ragged clothes. Barking "Git goin!" again and again, they trot him into the night. The port of entry glows to the east. A helicopter circles low in the distance, probing the land with its spotlight. There are no birds, crickets, or frogs. You hear the muted roar of the cities and the crunch of footsteps on gravel.

Two miles away along Interstate 5, human waves sweep across the freeway. Interstate 5 starts at the port of entry and heads north, through downtown San Diego and Los Angeles. It is lit, but the immigrants hide in the shadows, waiting for gaps in the traffic. Because some of them misjudge the speed of the oncoming cars, in recent years hundreds have been hit and killed. California has lowered the speed limits and installed flashing yellow lights above warning signs. The warning signs show figures immediately recognizable as immigrants—they run hunched over, they hold hands, and the women wear scarfs. But people drive fast in San Diego, rarely under seventy. A local driver said to me, "Gee, those poor Mexicans. You know who I'm more concerned about?"

I thought, let me guess.

He said, "The people who hit them. When you run out on the freeway, you make a choice. When you're *driving* the freeway, you have no choice. You go straight ahead or into the cars next to you."

"You could slow down . . ."

"They're causing people to have accidents," he said. "We ought to build a fence."

Most of the people who run onto the freeway go all the way across and melt into the city. But others stop halfway, along the freeway's concrete median strip. The median is neutral ground, where the Border Patrol will not chase them. By midnight several hundred people have gathered there, under the glare of overhead lights. They wait with their guides for prearranged rides or rest before moving on. They sleep, eat, play cards. I have watched them dancing. Some may have made love or given birth. At dawn you see those who are stuck, afraid to move on. Like any neutral ground, the median can be a trap as well as a haven.

Against this flux of humanity stand eight hundred border guards, a quarter of the entire Border Patrol. One guard said to me, "We could link hands out here and still we couldn't stop them." He was discouraged and bitter, the kind of man who could turn violent. A civil rights activist said, "I call them the bucket brigade. We should send them to the beach and have them empty the ocean. They would do just as good a job. They'd probably be happier." It's true that San Diego is an unhappy duty. It is a war of endless repetition fought on battlefields like Dairy Mart Road, McDonald's, and the parking lots of all the borderland motels.

The Border Patrol is the uniformed law-enforcement branch of the Immigration and Naturalization Service, the INS. It pays its guards poorly by San Diego standards but gives them job security. Many of the guards are recruited from the back-country towns of Texas and they have retained homespun names for the people they catch. "Wetback" is the most evocative: it brings to mind the Rio Grande, a late-night swim, the facelessness of a laborer stooping in a field. It is also a racial slur. Some years ago, orders came from headquarters that henceforth the cor-

rect term was to be "illegal alien." "Alien" suggested someone stranger than Mexican, but it bore the stamp of government and was hard to reduce to invective. "Illegal" was
more ominous: critics admitted that an act can be illegal
but wondered how a person can be. Washington compromised with yet another label, "undocumented alien." This
was one change too many for the guards, who are not
inclined to chase fashion. Some gave up saying "wetbacks"
only to take up "muds" instead. "Muds" is a short version
of "mud people," a white-supremacist term for all non-
European races. The use of such language is no more
surprising than the sentiment behind it. The Border Patrol
seems perfectly designed to incubate reactionary thought.
The guards are country boys given uniforms and a patri-
otic purpose, then assigned an impossible job. Society puts
them into what is essentially a racial fight, then wonders
at their frame of mind.

But it would be unfair to brand them all. A few border
guards sympathize openly with the immigrants. Most just
do their jobs and don't allow emotion to intervene. One
described it this way to me: "Catch 'em, write 'em up, back
to Mexico. Catch 'em, write 'em up, back to Mexico." In
recent years, they have written them up more than a
million times per year. That is the number of apprehensions, not immigrants. Because of the volume and the
difficulty of verifying identities, no record is kept of the
repeat business. The INS admits that the totals include
people who have been caught more than once in a fiscal
year. What it does not mention is that many have been
caught twice in a fiscal night. Still, the totals are not
complete nonsense: over the years they give a rough ac-

counting of the flow and measure the labor performed by the Border Patrol.

Ninety percent of the people caught are Mexicans. The other 10 percent are OTMs, which stands for "other than Mexicans," and means mostly Central and South Americans. The distinction is important, because OTMs cannot be shipped to Mexico and must be flown home. Deportation is a serious setback for them; it may be months before they can make the trip north again. Mexicans can move faster. They waive their right to a hearing, take the INS bus to the border, and if the night is young, turn around and come right back. Though the official estimate is that half or two thirds get through, the real numbers are higher. The truth is that everyone who persists eventually manages to enter the United States.

Some observers conclude that the border is wide open. A few even believe this is to be desired. I talked to an American in Tijuana, a libertarian who had moved there because, he said, "I weighed U.S. laws and Mexican laws, and decided that Mexican laws weigh less." He was a philosopher. He said, "The human animal is migratory by nature." He told me that he opposed the Border Patrol on principle and argued that an open border should be declared. He said, "The line is artificial. We have an open border anyway. Why not acknowledge reality?"

I argued something different: if the boundary is a fiction, it functions to the extent it is believed. People who understand neither the political nor geographic complexities of North America cannot imagine that the mighty United States could have difficulty enforcing its perimeter. Millions of desperate people are dissuaded by the simplest line on a map. But if the United States dropped even the pretense of border defense, those millions might change their minds. An avowedly open border would stir immigration on a scale that even California could not accommodate. As it is, the boundary acts as a filter crossed by the energetic and the brave. If the border is a myth, it is a useful one. The Border Patrol's real function is to play along.

A border guard told me a war story. He said, "I was on horse patrol. We caught a group and put them on the ground. There was this old woman, about seventy, who motioned to me. You know, 'Officer, ¡*Oficial!*'

"I go, 'What.'

"She had a four-year-old boy with her. She says, 'Do you know anybody who wants this kid?'

"I go, '*What?*'

"She was Salvadoran. She says, 'My son and daughter-in-law were killed, gunned down. I'm the only family this boy has. I figured I'd come up north, give him to somebody, give him a life. He's a good boy.' She says, 'Why don't *you* take him? You live well here.'

"He was a beautiful boy. If I could have stuck him in my pocket and taken him home, I would have raised him up. We can't do that. It's an impossibility. But I looked back at this old woman and she was desperate. Like, what's going to become of him?

"That happened nine years ago and I still think about it today. There are some desperate people who have some desperate reasons to come up here. Good reasons."

The border guard was the son of an immigrant, as am I.

He took a breath and said, "But so many people want to jump on the bandwagon and don't have the right reasons for coming here. When I started with the Border Patrol, the majority of the men I apprehended were between twenty-five and fifty. Now this is just a bunch of young . . ." He stopped himself. "We still catch men with families, but now you see a lot of juveniles, kids, guys seventeen, eighteen, twenty-one. They don't have any skills. They don't know what it is to work out in the fields. They go to Los Angeles and the big cities. Let's face it, they're young and they've got one-track minds: they just want to have a good time. They want to get a boom box, get some nice clothes, and party. To do that they've got to have money, and the best way to get money is dealing—prowling cars, dealing dope, getting into the fast lane."

If his emotions were contradictory, so are those of most Americans: in this nation built on immigration, each new surge has frightened us. As far back as 1750, after German farmers settled in Pennsylvania, Benjamin Franklin complained about their "political immaturity and social incivility," and wrote that "those who come hither are generally the most stupid of their own nation . . . not being used to liberty, they know not how to make a modest use of it." In *Observations Concerning the Increase of Mankind*, published in 1751, he asked, "Why should the Palatine Boors be suffered to swarm into our settlements and, by herding together, establish their language and manners to the exclusion of ours? Why should Pennsylvania, founded by the English, become a colony of aliens, who will shortly be so numerous as to germanize us instead of our own anglifying them, and will never adopt our language or customs, any more than they can acquire our complexion?"

Similar fears have surfaced about Africans, French, Irish, Chinese, Japanese, Greeks, Poles, and Italians—and most recently about Latin Americans. The concerns are not unreasonable. We worry that immigrants will change us, and they have.

The problem is that history cannot provide the absolute reassurance some might seek. While it is true that immigrants have constantly renewed the United States, it is equally true that each wave of immigration has been different. The current wave, in years of economic and social difficulty, has undeniably placed burdens on the nation. The list of our woes is familiar: rotten cities, resentful populations, bad government, and racial tensions. Impoverished immigrants do not cause these problems, but in the short term they add to them. The long term seems too far away. The similarity between today's nativist fears and those of the past does not prove they are unjustified. Few people would advocate the open-immigration policies that the United States maintained when travel was difficult and the nation was younger. No one knows the real consequences of Mexican immigration: it is a movement of the largest scale, infinitely complex, around which opposing arguments can easily be constructed. The view from San Diego is admittedly unnerving: these strangers may indeed be the ones we cannot accommodate. Our history, however, suggests otherwise.

Eighty thousand Spanish-speaking people remained in the Southwest when the United States acquired the territory after the war with Mexico. By the terms of the peace treaty, they were given citizenship and offered the full protection of the law. Full protection didn't amount to much. Within a few years, Mexican landholders had been stripped of their properties by predatory Anglos and unsympathetic courts. Few people were affected because the great majority of Mexicans lived as serfs and, upon becoming U.S. citizens, had nothing to lose.

A larger injustice was that almost overnight the Mexicans were made foreigners in their own land. Along with the Chinese, they were turned into the underclass of American westward expansion, scorned but needed. The need, of course, was for cheap and docile labor. The problem was that under the new masters, the West was industrializing rapidly, outpacing the domestic supply of workers. By the 1880s, employers were importing Mexican nationals by the thousands to build railroads and work in the fields, mines, and factories. In those years, the United States worried about the permeability of the southern border not because of Mexicans, but because of Chinese. Excluded by immigration reform in 1882, Asians were walking in the back door. Mexicans were considered preferable because they were less foreign and in theory could more easily be sent home when they were no longer needed. Despite the fact that many stayed, raised families, and became citizens—despite the fact that many were citizens to begin with—the idea of the Mexican as a temporary worker persisted.

In the 1920s, more than a half million arrived. Worried about unfair competition and the suppression of wages, labor unions led the fight for border restrictions. The

Border Patrol was formed in 1924, and five years later unauthorized entry into the United States became a crime. Then as now, the consequence of outlawing the immigrants was to force them deeper into the shadows and to further suppress U.S. wages. Perhaps the unions should have welcomed the Mexicans and recruited them. But when the Great Depression washed over the country, eliminating work at any price, Mexicans stopped coming anyway. Many who were here went home voluntarily, while thousands of others were rounded up and deported. For the first time in U.S. history, more people left the country than entered it.

The current wave of immigration began during World War II, when the United States again grew hungry for laborers. In 1942, the U.S. government extended a now notorious invitation, the Bracero program, by which temporary Mexican workers were imported under guarantees of a minimum wage and crude but livable housing. (Bracero means "helping arms.") At first, Texas farmers boycotted the program—they had plenty of Mexican workers already and they objected to the government's interference in the free market. Within a few years, however, it became clear that the guarantees to the workers were unenforceable and the farmers became eager participants. By the 1950s, the Bracero program was importing hundreds of thousands of seasonal farm workers. Even then the demand for labor outpaced the sanctioned supply and many workers slipped across the line illegally.

We crave cheap labor but fear the poor. At the height of the Bracero program in 1954, the Immigration Service launched Operation Wetback, a nationwide roundup that resulted in the repatriation of perhaps a million Mexicans. Intimidation lay at the heart of the operation; the government itself bragged about the numbers of Mexicans who had fled the country in fear. The man in charge was a retired army general, Joseph Swing, who had ridden on Pershing's frustrated expedition against Pancho Villa in 1916. This perhaps was his vengeance. Throughout the United States, the immigration squads hit the barrios and farms, invading homes and sweeping the streets for Mexicans. It was believed that you could tell a wetback by his rough clothes and humble demeanor. But many U.S. citizens were caught in the raids and some were deported. The public did not object. Concerned by the effect of Mexicans on U.S. wages, even the congressional liberals supported the deportations. It is a pattern repeated today. Then as now, the Mexicans simply turned around and came back.

When the Bracero program ended in 1964, the migrant labor tradition continued at full strength. Mexico's population had swollen and people needed jobs. They knew where to find them. The border itself was no longer a distant desert, but rather a string of familiar cities closely linked to the rest of Mexico by improved roads and public transport. Communication was improving, too. On television and in the movies, in letters home, the promised land lay near at hand.

In 1975 Leonard Chapman, commissioner of the INS, warned the nation about "a vast and silent invasion of illegal aliens." Chapman was another general, the former commandant of the marines. He reported that 12 million aliens had taken up residence and that most of them were

Mexican. He called for a Border Patrol of 200,000 guards, a force equal to his cherished Marine Corps. In 1978, former CIA Director William Colby asserted that Mexico was a greater threat than the Soviet Union. He predicted that 20 million unauthorized immigrants would infest the United States by the year 2000 and said (reasonably) that the only way to stop them was to develop Mexico's economy. Chapman and Colby were alarmists and their numbers were too high, but no one really knew how many immigrants had gone underground. By 1980, estimates ranged from 1 million to 6 million. The difference in opinion arose from one crucial question: Once the migrant workers crossed the border, how long did they stay?

In the fifties and sixties, perhaps 90 percent of the Mexican migrants were temporary. They were lone males, cowboys and farmworkers who traveled north each year, sent their earnings home, and dreamed perhaps of saving enough money to buy some land in Mexico. By the 1970s, the profile began to change. The farmers still came, but they were joined by increasing numbers of city dwellers looking for steadier work in manufacturing and the service industries. The city people stayed longer and melted more easily into the general population. Though most of them probably intended to return to Mexico, many were persuaded to settle by the material benefits. They began to bring in their families.

There is an old and circular argument about what drives illegal immigration: pressure from the south or suction from the north. The answer is both, sometimes more one than the other. Mexico's economic troubles in the 1980s—which reduced real wages by 40 percent—hit the country's cities hardest and accelerated changes already under way. More women and children came across. American bankers were not the only ones who had given up hope for Mexico: technicians, teachers, and graduate students joined the exodus.

In 1986, Congress passed the Immigration Reform and Control Act (IRCA). The new law, which recognized that immigration could not be stopped at the border, had two important provisions. The first outlawed the hiring of undocumented workers, closing the largest loophole in immigration law. Henceforth employees had to demonstrate their right to work and employers had to record this information on a form, called the I-9, for INS inspection. This part of the law was dubbed "employer sanctions," because it threatened fines and prison sentences for employers who did not comply. Civil libertarians labeled it a government intrusion into the workplace and fought off the call for a national identity card.

IRCA's second provision was legalization: it offered amnesty to immigrants who could prove that they had been living in the United States since 1982, and to others who were working in agriculture. Amnesty was not an act of charity but an acceptance of the facts. These people were entrenched, and difficult to identify. Large-scale deportations would have been cruel and politically unpalatable.

At first the new law seemed to work. Employers fired some people and filled in countless forms. The cost to society was high—in paperwork, and more ominously, in the public's acceptance of the procedures. For the sake of social discipline, the entire work force had to go on file. But the illegal back-and-forth traffic across the border did drop off. We now know why. Under the amnesty program more than three million people emerged from the shadows to claim permanent residence. Three quarters of them were Mexican, and they stayed in the United States while their applications were pending, rather than making the occasional trip to Mexico and back, which had been the usual pattern. Fearing that the traditional arrangement had finally ended, those who did not qualify for amnesty waited on either side of the border for the dust to settle. They need not have worried. A black market in phony documents sprang up to fill the need. It was a perfectly tailored solution—the kind of spontaneous adaptation that in other circumstances we admire. For a few dollars anyone could buy a Social Security card, a permanent-residence card, or a birth certificate. At first the counterfeits were crude; by now many are indistinguishable from the real thing. Either way, employers are off the hook and IRCA has collapsed. Renewed calls for a tamperproof identity card, this time to be combined with a national employee data base, again raise questions of civil liberties.

The United States sanctions more immigration than any other nation. During the 1980s, more than 6 million people were granted permanent U.S. residency, a figure exceeded only in the first decade of this century, when some nine million people were accepted. It is illuminating to weigh these numbers against the total population: from 1901 to 1910, the average annual number of immigrants per thousand U.S. residents was 10.4; in the 1980s, it was 2.7. However, these figures apply only to authorized immigration. At the start of the century almost all the immigrants came by ship and illegal immigration was insignificant. By contrast, in the 1980s, the majority of immigrants came across the southern border. Despite the legalization allowed by IRCA, a large underground population undoubtedly added to the weight of immigration.

By 1989, illegal crossings had again begun to increase, and by the early 1990s, they had approached pre-IRCA levels. Currently the INS estimates that the resident population of undocumented immigrants has climbed back to four million. Some scholars disagree, placing the number closer to two million. It is partly a political argument: the INS and its allies among the anti-immigrant coalitions want to whip up a scare; scholars tend to be sympathetic to the immigrants and they worry about the public's overreaction. As has always been the case, the issue makes for strange bedfellows: trade unionists and liberals join with racists and nationalists in opposing immigration, while mainstream conservatives and businesspeople join with civil rights activists in advocating a policy of acceptance. No one knows the real numbers. Surveys indicate that the trends of the 1970s have continued: in California, Arizona, and Texas, perhaps only 15 percent of Mexican immigrants now work in agriculture. Nationwide, families are reuniting around the men legalized by IRCA. Mutual aid networks are well developed and the pull runs deep through Mexico. Many Mexicans believe that the United States must once again grant amnesty.

Some analysts argue that the United States must let the border function as a pressure-relief valve, to give the Mexicans time to turn their economy around and to allow free trade an opportunity to work. They say Mexicans prefer Mexico and will stay there if their economy develops. It is a good theory, but there is evidence that Mexicans will not cooperate. To the extent that Mexico's economic growth is linked to the United States, it will continue to be concentrated along the border. As still greater numbers of workers are drawn to northern Mexico and as their material expectations increase, the United States may continue to appear not less but more desirable. The lesson of Tijuana is that the flow of immigrants may actually increase. Despite their denials, true free traders must in their hearts accept this possibility, the human exchange, as part of the package.

The thought of human exchange of one kind or another is what frightens the most zealous nativists. Dr. John Tanton, the ophthalmologist who founded the English-only movement, recently wrote, "In this society, will the present majority peaceably hand over its political power to a group that is simply more fertile? Can *homo contraceptivus* compete with *homo progenitivo* if our borders aren't controlled? . . . Perhaps this is the first instance in which those with their pants up are going to get caught by those with their pants down. As whites see their power and control over their lives declining, will they simply go quietly into the night?" In Washington, D.C., a high INS official put it to me just as bluntly: "We're tired of serving as the dumping ground for a bunch of promiscuous half-breed Mexicans." I assumed by "we" he meant he and his friends.

Such concerns are not unique to the United States. The Japanese are famous for their racial anxieties. In Europe, which once tried to form the globe to its image, the feeling now is that the world has suddenly grown too small.

When I recently suggested to an otherwise polite class in a French lycée that Algerian immigration might be good for the country, I encountered overt hostility. It was nothing, of course, compared to the hostility that the Algerians themselves encounter. Nor are such concerns unique to our time. Benjamin Franklin wrote:

> . . . the number of purely white people in the world is proportionally very small. All Africa is black or tawney. Asia chiefly tawney. America (exclusive of the newcomers) wholly so. And in Europe, the Spaniards, Italians, French, Russians and Swedes, are generally of what we call a swarthy complexion; as are Germans also, the Saxons only excepted, who with the English, make the principal body of white people on the face of the earth. I could wish their numbers were increased. And while we are, as I may call it, *scouring* our planet, by clearing America of woods, and so making this side of our globe reflect a brighter light to the eyes of inhabitants of Mars or Venus, why should we in the sight of superior beings, darken its people? Why increase the sons of Africa, by planting them in America, where we have so fair an opportunity, by excluding all Blacks and Tawneys, of increasing the lovely white and red? But perhaps I am partial to the complexion of my country, for such kind of partiality is natural to mankind.

It would be unfair to judge Franklin by his choice of words. He wrote at a time when it was possible to speak openly about such matters. Were he writing now, no doubt he would choose a more guarded form of expression.

The most effective of the current anti-immigrant organizations have learned never to talk of race. But when they say *immigrant,* they mostly mean the brown-skinned Spanish-speaking variety. When pressed, they expand the definition to include Asians and Caribbean blacks. Immigrants are blamed for a wide range of woes, from the shortage of water to the decay of the Protestant ethic, from suburban sprawl and environmental degradation to bad schools. Sensing a winning issue, elected officials articulate more mainstream objections: they blame immigrants for competing with the poor, burdening state and local budgets, and crowding public services. It is a well established pattern: when society hurts, anti-immigrant sentiment grows.

The resentment has led to calls for sealing the border. This could be done—for instance, with a large-scale deployment of the U.S. armed forces and the creation of free-fire zones. It would not take much killing. The Soviets sealed their borders for decades without an excessive expenditure of ammunition. A systematic policy of shoot on sight would deter the Mexicans. But adopting such a policy is not a choice most Americans would make. It would immediately raise the question of what remained of the United States worth defending. This is, of course, part of a larger truth about national self-preservation: it takes courage not to indulge our fears.

Our fears are what worry Roberto Martínez, a Chicano activist and the Border Patrol's harshest critic. Martínez does not smile often or laugh easily. He works in San Diego for the American Friends Service Committee, the Quakers, and monitors civil rights violations along the border. He asked me not to call him Hispanic and explained that he is not Spanish but mestizo. There is no denying Martínez's Indian blood. At fifty-five, he is a stocky man with heavy jowls, copper skin, and a large, flat face. His hair is jet black. He dresses stodgily in a shirt and tie, wears thick glasses, and complains that his vision is changing so fast his optometrist can't keep up. His key chain reads WORLD'S GREATEST GRANDPA. He speaks gently and pursues his work with a single-mindedness that can make him seem distracted.

I asked about the economic changes in Mexico and he apologized. "I haven't given it much thought. I'm so busy here, you see." By "here" he meant his downtown office—a small, well-lit room with none of the clutter of a movement headquarters. Martínez does not advertise or go looking for trouble. He sits at his desk with a telephone and a computer, and trouble finds him. In San Diego and Tijuana it is common knowledge that people who are beaten by Mexican authorities have no recourse, but people who are beaten by the Americans, or have their rights trampled on, can turn to Roberto Martínez. He is not a lawyer, but a professional witness who came up from the streets. He will not be intimidated. He complains, agitates, publicizes. He is unreasonably persistent. He sues. The agents of law enforcement scorn him. They are dedicated men and women in a difficult situation, and Martínez reins them in. The fact that he can is one difference between Mexico and the United States. In this peculiar way Martínez is an American patriot.

He keeps photo albums of his clients, men and women with battered faces, bruised bodies, broken bones, gunshot wounds. The photographs are gruesome and in color.

They give the albums the appearance of the Mexican magazines that revel in highway accidents. The people in them are mestizos. They look stunned, unhappy, belligerent, afraid. Martínez remembers all their stories:

This one was caught just after he came over the fence. He ran and they chased him down.

This one was sixteen. He picked up a rock and they shot him in the gut.

They caught him at a checkpoint up north on the interstate. They tried to get him to sign a voluntary return. He refused and said he wanted a hearing before an immigration judge. They took him to the back room and beat him until he signed.

They assaulted her sexually in front of her husband and child. They called it a body search and spread-eagled her on the ground. Her husband sobbed, "Tolerate it; you will have your day."

Martínez can sound obsessed. His problem is that the stories quickly become repetitive and the public is unsympathetic. Local television stations and newspapers have grown reluctant to cover his press conferences, not because they doubt him, but because they have heard it all before. The Border Patrol dismisses him with a shrug: "Martínez again, with another one of his unsubstantiated allegations." And the victims themselves are reluctant to testify. They come from countries where police abuse is the norm and they don't want trouble. They broke the law by entering the country. The protections guaranteed by the U.S. Constitution do not impress them. They want to get on with their lives.

One morning last summer, in the hours before dawn,

a Guatemalan woman named Marta came across with a group at San Ysidro. She was twenty-two years old, unmarried, and five months pregnant. When the Border Patrol surprised them, Marta began screaming, *"La Migra! Run! Run!"* Martínez told me this.

One of the guards lost his temper, grabbed Marta, and threw her furiously to the ground. She kept screaming and he clubbed her repeatedly with a heavy flashlight until she was quiet. An ambulance was called. The guard accompanied Marta to the hospital and warned her not to file a complaint. Five hours later she lost her baby. Afterward she was sent to an alternative detention center, run by Catholic nuns, where a man in civilian clothes again advised her to keep quiet. Believing she might be made to "disappear," she lay terrified in her cell. Finally her cell mate, a Mexican woman, telephoned Martínez. It took him two days, but he convinced her to file a complaint. Suddenly she was moved to another detention center and then on to the big facility in Los Angeles. She called Martínez from there, but the phone was yanked from her hand. Within days she was flown to Guatemala. Martínez managed to phone her there and she said she had changed her mind: since she intended to return to the United States, she would not complain. Martínez, in other words, had lost his case.

He wins often enough, however, to provoke angry reactions from the San Diego public. Threats by telephone and mail punctuate his life. For instance:

ROBERTO, YOU DIRTY FUCKING SPIC GREASER. YOU BETTER
START KEEPING YOUR MOUTH SHUT ABOUT YOUR GREASE TRIBE

COMING OVER THE BORDER, YOU BEANERS GOT NO BUSINESS DEFENDING THIS. THIS ILLEGAL CROSSING HAS BEEN GOING ON TOO LONG, AND WHITE POWER IS NOT GOING TO LET YOU HAVE ANY POLITICAL CLOUT OVER IT, SO YOU BETTER SHUT UP, BUDDY, YOU ARE COMING DOWN TO YOUR TIME NOW. THE COPS ARE GOING TO START SHOOTING YOU MEXICANS WHOLESALE SOON, AND THERE WILL BE NOTHING YOU CAN DO ABOUT IT . . . SORRY, ROBERTO, YOU CAN'T HAVE CALIFORNIA BACK, YOU DON'T DESERVE IT. THE WHITE MAN BUILT THIS NATION AND YOU GREASERS ARE GUESTS, UNTIL WE DECIDE WHAT TO DO WITH YOU . . . STOP CRITICIZING THE BORDER PATROL AND THE WHITES WHO ARE TRYING TO SAVE OUR WHITE COUNTRY . . . WE ARE GOING TO CHOKE ALL YOU PACHOOKOS, VATO MARICONE. DIG IT BABY, YOU HAVE WORN OUT YOUR WELCOME, ESSE'. WHITE POWER IS GOING TO GET YOU, CHUKO.

Martínez keeps his home phone unlisted and does not advertise the location of his office. His employers at the American Friends Service Committee have installed an expensive burglar alarm in his house. But as Martínez knows, there can be no assurance of safety.

Surprisingly, his biggest fear is of the Border Patrol. Early one evening, at dusk, we took a ride along the boundary fence. He said, "The Border Patrol is the most uncontrolled, unsupervised, and undisciplined law-enforcement agency in the country. They think they are above the law. They think they can get away with anything."

I prodded him. "But would they want to?"

"They have a gang mentality, a turf thing, and they act on each other. They have a code of silence, a code of revenge. They will always cover up."

We parked by an abandoned quarry and watched the first large groups running north. A Border Patrol van cruised by us. Martínez looked tense. "I don't come here much anymore," he said. "Especially once the sun's gone down. My wife worries."

"About crime?" I asked, not understanding.

He shook his head and checked the rearview mirror. "About the Border Patrol. They recognize me. Some of them would like nothing better than to catch me alone out here."

"There are two of us tonight."

"They come to my house, you know. They blow their horns. They stop across the street and videotape me. They park transport vans there and load them with people. They look into my windows with binoculars. They come into my driveway."

I asked him if, given his way, he would eliminate the Border Patrol. The question was obvious, but it seemed to surprise him. He answered, "Eliminate? We should work toward reducing . . . toward eliminating? At the very least toward *disarming* them."

We drove north in silence. I watched Martínez's face in profile, lit for a moment by an oncoming car. His expression was heavy. In blackness he said, "You don't run, you don't argue, and you don't refuse to sign. You don't assert yourself. You do whatever they say. Even if you are a citizen, you have no rights."

Martínez is a fifth-generation Mexican-American. He was born in 1937 to parents who had fled the dismal life of West Texas. He grew up in the barrios at the heart of San Diego.

His family was poor but large. They owned the ramshackle Victorian house where Martínez lives today. As a boy he worked in the fields, traveling with his parents to the labor camps of the San Joaquin and Salinas valleys. He was harassed on buses by soldiers who said, "Hey, you must be one of those *pachucos.*" He remembers the zoot suit riots of 1942, when bands of U.S. Navy sailors roamed Los Angeles and San Diego hunting young Chicanos. The zoot suit was a ghetto way of dressing—a broad-shouldered tapered-leg costume worn with a long chain and a wide-brimmed hat. To the farmboys serving in the navy during a time of war and conformity, the suit marked the otherness of city blacks and Chicanos. To the Anglo-Saxon establishment of southern California, it stood for rebellion. When the disturbances broke out, the police stood by and the *Los Angeles Times* blamed barrio youths for the violence, implying that by their antisocial behavior they had provoked the attacks. But it was not the zoot suiters who rioted. Martínez hid with his family. The disturbances lasted several days, and ended after the navy confined its sailors to their ships.

Martínez lost an uncle to the war. His father returned wounded from the South Pacific and took to drinking. In the 1950s, the barrios were hit by Immigration Service raids and repatriations, and Martínez, now a teenager, lived under the constant threat of being deported. The fact that he was American did not reassure him—in some ways, it only heightened his fear. "I had no relatives in Mexico. I didn't speak much Spanish. They might as well have sent me to China." They sent him nowhere but kept him worried. When he was fourteen and still in school, he found work washing dishes in downtown restaurants. The jobs rarely lasted long. Most of the other workers were immigrant Mexicans, and on several occasions informants called the Border Patrol before payday and had the entire kitchen staff hauled off. The police were worse. They would pull up beside Martínez on the street, shove him against a wall, point a gun to his head, handcuff him, and take him to jail. It was an almost weekly routine. They had composite drawings of thieves, and all Mexicans looked the same. Martínez was never formally charged. At school he was put into "adjustment classes," where he did not adjust. A counselor advised him not to graduate, and explained, "We need laborers."

I asked how he had felt about the treatment.

He said, "I thought they must be doing this to everyone. It must be normal."

His cousins began using heroin. His older brother turned to drink, and repeatedly served time in juvenile detention for street crimes. Martínez still cannot speak about him easily. "My brother was headed for destruction," he told me sadly. "I knew it then—he had given up on himself. I was different. I was interested in painting and music. I had a force, a vitality that had to come out. My brother had nothing. He died in 1957 in a car wreck on his twenty-first birthday. These kinds of things shape your life. You try to forget, but these things come back to haunt you."

Martínez's parents did not encourage him to study. He dropped out of school when he was seventeen, got a job in a sliding-lock factory, and later went to work for an airplane manufacturer. He married and began to have children. Eventually he had five. He was laid off at the factory, rehired, laid off, rehired—the endless cycle of an unskilled laborer. He decided to enroll in night school. I asked him why. He looked at me as if to say, this is obvious. "I saw how hard life was on the production line. I saw how hard life was off of it, in the barrio. I wanted to get ahead. I wanted to assimilate."

The day he got his high school degree, he walked across the street and enrolled in a community college. He graduated with a degree in technical design. He rose through the ranks at work and earned the title of engineer. By the mid-1960s, he had risen far enough to leave the inner city. It was a chance to remove his children from the poverty and violence of the streets, and give them a good education. The place he chose was Santee, a white middle-class suburb about fifteen miles inland.

The locals call it "East County." It is a district of run-together towns sprawling through desert valleys. I asked Martínez what kind of people live there and he answered, "Ex-military types, retirees, the kind of people who want good weather, the kind who move to paradise."

These are San Diego's other immigrants. Many come from the Midwest. Their yards are planted with midwestern lawns and aspiring trees. Because the neighborhoods are slapped together quickly and without regard to the surrounding landscape, they have a temporary and fragile appearance. More care has been put into making the churches seem permanent. There are large congregations with impressive facades—mostly Protestant and Christian fundamentalist.

Life in East County is something many Californians know about. The climate is sometimes too hot or too cold, except in the shopping malls. Residents drive from home to store in four-wheel-drive pickups and climb the hillsides on Japanese dirt bikes. A wooden sign festooned with civic club seals reads LAKESIDE——A FRIENDLY PLACE TO LIVE. It is impossible to tell if the sign marks the start, the end, or the center of town. The streets have names like sales slogans: Orange Crest and Palm Glen, Buena Vista and Los Ranchitos, Peaceful Court and Carefree Drive. There are few sidewalks and fewer pedestrians. The parks are empty and unappealing. The downtowns never existed. People eye each other on the freeway and drive on. An exaggerated fear of crime can bring them together for an occasional evening with a community-service policeman. Otherwise, they share the parallel experience of television in solitude. It does not give them much to talk about. While driving, they listen to the radio. A visitor senses the isolation most strongly. Access to the freeway is too easy. With a single wrong turn, you can end up on the interstate merged into fast-moving traffic, like an unwanted stranger being escorted out of town.

Martínez's new house was a three-bedroom box on a corner lot. He bought it with a rent-to-own arrangement, figuring his biggest problem would be meeting the payments. He did not even consider that people might resent the arrival of nonwhites.

"In a strange way, living in the barrio insulates you from the realities of race," he told me. The same, of course, holds for whites who live in the wealthy suburbs. But Santee was never wealthy. Someone broke into the new house and carved slogans into the simulated paneling on the walls. FUCKING WETBACKS. GO BACK WHERE YOU CAME FROM.

Across the street, a black family fled after a cross was burned on their lawn. Martínez and his family had second thoughts, but they stuck it out. Other Mexican-Americans arrived from the barrio and tensions grew. You need a *them* to have an *us*: race was giving the people of Santee an unintended sense of community.

Martínez joined a Chicano social group, at first to share music and language. Under attack by the society of East County, the group changed and started to concern itself with questions of fairness and self-defense. Martínez developed a reputation as a leader. In the early 1970s the situation worsened. The Youth Klan Corps began recruiting in the schools and distributing anti-Mexican literature. One afternoon a woman called Martínez to say that fighting had broken out at the high school that his children attended. Chicanos had been beaten by Anglo gangs armed with two-by-fours. The police had arrived and were arresting the victims. It was the zoot suit riots all over again.

I asked Martínez to show me the school. We drove to Santee and parked across the street. The buildings were large, modern, and unimpressive. It was the end of the school day. Most of the students who streamed by us were mestizo, though whites mixed in. Martínez watched them impassively. He said, "You see how it's changed. Back then we were just a few. Those are the fields where the fights happened. If you can call them fights. It's like calling Wounded Knee a battle."

"How did you react?"

"I got angry. People aren't born with a social conscience, you know. It's something that gets pounded into you. Santee was the second time around for me. It opened the floodgates."

Martínez fought back with growing insistence. He protested, petitioned, and sought legal advice. As the confrontations worsened, the school officials took the side of the Anglos and the police spread the pressure into the neighborhoods. There were break-ins, raids, and arrests. Martínez served as the focal point of resistance. He began to win lawsuits against the police, victories that gave people courage and hope. Slowly the tensions eased. By then Martínez's reputation had spread throughout the Mexican community of San Diego. Chicanos and immigrants from the entire county were coming to him and pleading for his help. Stunned by the level of despair and encouraged by his Catholic faith, he knew he had found his calling. In 1977, he quit his job as an engineer and went to work full time as a community organizer. Five years later, after a divorce, he left Santee. He remarried and moved back into his family's old house. He thought that living in the barrio would make him a more credible witness to the suffering of his people.

The barrio has grown rougher and more transient. When Martínez was a boy, he heard English on the streets; now he hears only Spanish. Many of the new residents are first-generation immigrants, and some have come illegally. Tensions with the police and Border Patrol are at an all-time high. The tight weave of the city poses problems for officers who are supposed to enforce the immigration laws. Can Border Patrol guards judge a man's immigration status by the dirt on his shoes? Can they judge a woman by the color of her lips? They cannot, of course, but they must. As a result, large populations of legitimate U.S.

residents live under conditions of official suspicion and police harassment. They are detained by the hundreds, and because of the overall quality of forgeries, some are deported to Mexico. No statistics are kept, but given the intensity of the INS presence in the barrio, it is likely that such mistakes are as common now as during the peak years of Operation Wetback. Only the language has changed.

In INS terminology, a "raid" became a "sweep," then a "survey." Martínez tells what happens when surveys go wrong: a girl is rounded up on her way to school and sent to Mexico; a family is torn apart; there are beatings, suicides, and unexplained deaths in jail. A third of Martínez's clients are Americans. He himself no longer draws a distinction between resident and alien, or between barrio and border. As he points out, immigration issues inevitably become race issues, and a war against illegal immigration becomes a war against ourselves.

As Martínez drove me through the neighborhoods, he said, "They hit this place hard, day after day. They give no one the benefit of the doubt. They bust into people's houses without warrants. They rip up legitimate documents. They use German shepherds and stun guns, undercover agents and assault teams. They fly helicopters overhead. Now they want rubber bullets." He was talking about the Border Patrol and the municipal police. The agencies work closely together. Until Martínez put a stop to it, in nearby National City even the dogcatcher wore a gun and hunted Mexicans.

This is the other war zone, and it is the center of San Diego: sprawling districts of vacant lots, weathered houses, and liquor stores with bars on the doors and windows. It is a land of knife wounds and drive-by shootings. Gang graffiti covers weathered walls. The sense of siege is undeniable. At the center stands the San Diego Police headquarters, an imposing blue-steel building, seven stories tall, with a rooftop helipad and fortified command bunker. It looks down on the neighborhoods from behind mirrored windows.

Martínez took me to the anniversary celebration of Chicano Park, a grassy lot in the shade of entwined freeway overpasses. The police seemed as numerous as the celebrants. A band in a pavilion chanted rap songs. Radical Chicanos from as far away as Los Angeles had set up booths to distribute their literature. They made it clear that as an Anglo, I was not welcome. Martínez said, "They go too far sometimes." A famous poster showed a frowning Aztec pointing like Uncle Sam and asking, "Who's the illegal immigrant, Pilgrim?" I listened to the speeches, which were full of bravura and defiance but oddly hopeless, as if the speakers understood that their displays of unity would not solve the problems of the barrio. By dusk, rival gangs had gathered at opposite ends of the park. Martínez got me away before the fighting began.

On the next block a tousle-haired kid was being handcuffed and held against a tree by policemen wearing gloves. His eyes were confused. The policemen found a knife in one pocket and a hypodermic needle in another. Martínez watched until they had finished searching him, then he turned away and said sadly, "This will be the last celebration at Chicano Park. Drugs have sapped Chicano pride." Gangs and alcohol, too.

We drove into the night. Young men loitered on the corners, watching us sullenly. In one district Martínez grew nervous. "Roll up your window and lock your door; a white man's not safe, even with me. They'll drag you out of the car. They'll kill you just for looking."

A brown man's not safe either. Martínez drove me to see the house where he was born. It was up a black alley, which he did not dare enter. Rolling through a red light, he said, "You don't stop. You just hope the car doesn't break down." We went to see the school he had attended, but the street was blocked by squad cars. A body lay facedown in the gutter, swept by flashing lights.

Martínez said, "You see what we do to ourselves?"

We parked to watch the crowds at the trolley station, on the line from the border. He said, "Now here's another generation growing up with no respect for the law. They see their fathers beaten and humiliated. They see them zapped, three, four times. They see the doors kicked in and the houses trashed. They see their neighbors hauled away." Speaking of his work, he said, "We're realistic, you know. We don't put any faith in the complaint process. We go through all this to show the police and the Border Patrol that we know what's going on."

One Saturday evening I went out with the Border Patrol in San Ysidro. I signed a liability release, but there was no danger—this was the Cook's tour of the combat zone. My guide was one of the supervisors, an affable Puerto Rican from Manhattan named Norbert Gomez. He spoke with a New York accent and had a habit of asking open-ended questions:

"An alien sees me, what's the first thing that goes through his mind?"

I forget the exact answer, but it was something like "friendship" or "respect." Gomez saw the world in his image. He had the swagger and self-confidence of the streets.

He took me to the port of entry and spoke a few words to the hustlers playing cards on the steps. They mumbled and looked away. Gomez said, "These guys here, they're big shots because they can come up to my car and extend their hand out, and I'll shake their hand."

I didn't think they looked like the type.

Gomez wanted to show me the boundary before sunset. We drove east along the fence in a standard-issue Bronco, caged in the back to hold prisoners. Looking down into Mexico from a small rise, Gomez swept his hand and said, "Tijuana, Tee Jay, The Quick Fix." Then he, too, asked me to roll up my window. "They throw rocks," he said. "Those are some bad *colonias* over there. We find dead bodies hung out on the fence."

He told me how he was raised: "Grow up. Go to the army. Get out. Get a job. Vote. Be a good person." He wanted to be a cop in New York but became one in San Diego, and then transferred to the Border Patrol. "I'm a happy man," he said, and, still driving, grabbed a sandwich from the boxed dinner on his lap. "I got a beautiful wife. Gorgeous. A knockout. Used to be a model."

We drove to the desert on the outskirts of the cities. Where the fence ended, the boundary was marked by a steel cable strung between posts. The cable was meant to prevent cars from driving across, but it had been cut. Ahead a family walked along the track, followed by two black mongrels.

Gomez interpreted the situation for me. He said, "Their

intention is not to enter the United States but to walk their dogs."

We turned back toward the port of entry and came upon two small boys. Gomez motioned them over and gave them the remainder of his meal. We drove on and he shuffled through a stack of papers. "Last year in this sector alone we apprehended 472,323 aliens. Our monthly average was 39,360. This year, the average is running over 45,000."

"You mean apprehensions, not people," I said.

He waved away the difference. "If you want action, this job's better than the E ticket at Disneyland." He got back to the numbers. Seized: 13,000 pounds of marijuana, 681.23 pounds of cocaine, 114.5 pounds of heroin, 50 weapons, 630 vehicles. OTMs this month: 228 Salvadorans, 75 Guatemalans, 48 Hondurans, 8 Chinese.

"Chinese?" I asked. Still?

"Chinese, Rumanians, Brazilians, Africans, Russians, Pakistanis. Mexico is an open visa. You never know what's coming over the fence."

Night fell, black and cold, and we drove into the badlands east of the port of entry. Gomez had deployed twenty-three men there, to guard three miles of boundary. At the top of a hill we stood with a two-man team working an infrared scope. They were laconic country boys in camouflage jackets. They radioed the other agents and directed them to their quarry: below you, ten yards west, behind the rock, hiding in the grass. I looked through the scope into a bright greenish landscape of gullies and bushes, and watched the phosphorescent figures moving north. I thought, in Vietnam we would have called in air strikes, and we didn't win there either.

Gomez grew more intense as the night wore on. In a dark canyon we walked away from the Bronco. He switched off his flashlight, and we stood in silence. He whispered, "You're an agent out here alone. What do you see?"

"Nothing."

The bushes rustled. He whispered, "Animal or alien?"

I didn't answer.

He nudged me, "What about your nose?"

I hesitated.

He said, "Did you know you can actually smell the presence of aliens?"

He switched on the light. "You see, out here a Border Patrol agent has to use all his senses."

But in San Ysidro the job seemed like fishing in an overstocked pond. The agents were hauling in would-be immigrants by the dozen. As a demonstration, Gomez called over the helicopter, which lit up a group for us. Two did not run. Gomez greeted them, frisked them, and ushered them gently into the back of the Bronco. They were men in their thirties with wild hair and soiled clothes, as if they had traveled far. They seemed stunned but not afraid. Gomez wrinkled his nose. "Whew, these guys are ripe."

We drove them out of the hills. I did not want to feed on their misfortune. I asked them how they felt, and they said okay. They said they would try again later in the night. For my benefit Gomez asked, "Who do you like better, the *Migra* or the Mexican police?" They said the

Migra—the U.S. immigration police—and I did not doubt them.

In a busy parking lot by the port of entry we handed them over to the transport units, and then we turned and watched at least a hundred more people cresting the hill above us. The helicopter clattered furiously, stabbing the line with its light. Border Patrol trucks churning dust fanned out to meet the onslaught. Through the confusion, apparently unaware, walked groups of college students going south to drink in Tijuana. Gomez smiled at three pretty girls and said, "You take care over there," and they giggled.

We met another agent, an immaculate man with a starched uniform and a narrow, pale face. He spoke about San Ysidro. "Your basic lower middle class. It's not a bad neighborhood per se; it's just that it has its trouble with the alien traffic." His pronunciation was careful. He told me he had a master's degree in sociology. "We hear a lot of complaints—your beatings, your civil rights cases, what have you. When you deal with this volume of custodial arrests, you just have to figure on that. It does not get me excited."

But Gomez worried it. We drove back out into the desert and parked, and he said, "The Border Patrol this, the Border Patrol that. There's people who think all we do is beat on Mexicans. Did you know that we get only one allegation for every seventeen thousand arrests?"

I had heard the number already from Roberto Martínez, who believes it says more about the stoicism of the immigrants than about the conduct of the Border Patrol. I didn't know how to answer Gomez without seeming accusatory.

He read my silence anyway and asked, "What's an agent to do, not defend himself? Put yourself in our position. You're out here doing your job, you apprehend some aliens, a fight ensues, someone picks up a rock. A rock can kill you. It can render you unconscious. It can take your eye out. It's a missile, just like a bullet. People will say, how can you put a gun up against a rock? Well, let me throw a rock at you. I'll put a gun in your hand and you tell me when you're ready to shoot."

"They must have knives, too," I said helpfully.

"Knives, pistols. Out here, you walk up on a bunch of people, you don't know who they are or what they're carrying. You've got a criminal element coming across who know just how to take you down."

He had me stand against his truck with my hands on the roof and my legs spread apart. "Like in the movies, right?" He walked up behind, as if to frisk me, and said, "Jab me with your arm, then reach across and grab my gun." I jabbed him in pantomime and touched his holster. Now he had me stand with my fingers interlocked over my head. He came up behind from an unexpected angle and squeezed my hands hard. He said, "You cannot put yourself at ease at any time." I was immobilized with pain. I thought he might snap my fingers. But he was not antagonistic; he wanted me to understand.

Fifty miles above the border, on the rolling plain between San Diego and Los Angeles, the Country Store stands beside a busy highway. It was founded by a chicken farmer back in the days when northern San Diego was still genuine farm country. Recently, however, the area's main crop has been new housing. Seen from the hills, developments sprout in the fields in a patchwork that extends to the horizons. The change has come so fast that even teenagers regret the passing of open land. The chicken farmer has retired rich. The remaining farmers grow strawberries, vegetables, and ornamental shrubs while awaiting their turns.

The store sells fresh fruit and processed groceries along with delicatessen meats, salads, coffees, and overstuffed sandwiches. The "Country" in its name is mostly packaging, a piece of theater immortalized by a giant fiberglass chicken on the roof. The chicken is a touch of genius: in a land of peculiar blandness, it gives people a point of reference and makes the store famous. This is equally true among immigrant workers, the thousands of Mexicans living in squatters' camps between the housing developments. Many are impoverished Mixtec Indians from the state of Oaxaca. They choose this area because there is work here and because it lies south of the Border Patrol checkpoint on the freeway at San Clemente. Since they do not speak or read English, they call the store "La Gallina," after the chicken. They walk miles to it. Mornings, they gather by the dozens in the parking lot and wait for employers to hire them for day jobs. The home owners, contractors, and farmers who take advantage of their offer generally pay minimum wage and do not abuse the workers. The Mexicans are dirty from living in the fields but usually well-mannered and subservient. They spend freely in the store on food and beer, and by most measures they are good customers. It seems surprising that the storekeepers despise them. But the store, like the half-country around it, has outgrown the need for Mexicans.

The storekeepers are two brothers named Randy and Rickey Ryberg. They are tall, burly men in their mid-thirties. Roberto Martínez, who has despised them for years, calls them "bruisers." The brothers tower over the immigrants and do not hide their anger. Insisting that their establishment is private property, they run Mexicans out of the store. They chase them away from the public telephones. They run them off the parking lot. They would run them out of the county and out of the country if they could.

Early one morning in 1990, a migrant named Candido Salas walked into the store to buy a cup of coffee. Salas was a slight Mixtec who had crossed the border illegally at San Ysidro and had been working in the fields for four months. Randy Ryberg collared Salas, accused him of coming to steal, and with the help of a butcher named Zimmerman, dragged him to the back of the store. They bound him with duct tape and handcuffed him to a railing. It was alleged that they also beat him. Rickey Ryberg, the older brother, came along, saw the captive, and walked away. Apparently a Border Patrol guard saw him, too, and left without asking questions. After several hours the men put a bag over Salas's head. They drew a clown's face on the bag and wrote NO MAS AQUI, crude Spanish for "Don't come back." Then they marched Salas, still bound with tape, into a field behind the store. Salas prepared to die. But his captors left him to wander blindly.

Migrants later claimed that the Rybergs had captured and terrorized other men before Salas. Grateful simply for being alive, fearful of the police and the Border Patrol, the victims had kept quiet. Salas was different. He went to the police. To a reporter from the *Los Angeles Times,* he said, "I want to prosecute because if we let this case go, they might one day kill one of my companions. If we stop here, the police won't pay any more attention to us. They'll say we're not serious enough to pursue these cases."

His concerns were legitimate. The migrants of northern San Diego inhabit an underworld where protection under the law is at best an abstraction. In recent years they have quietly endured hundreds, perhaps thousands, of attacks. With few complaints to act on, the police have taken little action. This in turn has reinforced the idea, widespread in San Diego, that immigrants are fair game. On the back roads near the squatters' camps, gangs of schoolboys armed with baseball bats threaten and rob the Mexicans. When the schoolboys grow up, some graduate to more serious actions. There have been killings.

Late one night, a short distance from the Country Store, two teenagers went out in a pickup truck to hunt Mexicans. When asked why later, the triggerman answered because he "didn't like them." His name was Kovzelove. He had close-cropped hair and a narrow face. Hunting Mexicans was not difficult for him. He found a pair walking in the dirt along a road called Black Mountain. Rising suddenly in the back of the pickup, firing a rifle and screaming "Die!" he killed both of them. Later he admitted to the police that he wished "there were forty of them, and they just rushed me, so that I could go off on everybody." It is difficult even to write about such feelings.

After Salas complained, the police reluctantly arrested the Ryberg brothers and the butcher. Like other shopkeepers, the Rybergs had friends on the force. The *Los Angeles Times* interviewed a detective, who said, "They were frustrated, pure and simple, but I don't think this thing has any racist overtones. This thing is a two-way street. A businessman loses thousands of dollars a year to shoplifters, people scaring away his good customers." Civil rights activists were outraged. If the attack on Salas had no racial overtones, it was driven by a hatred for the unwashed foreigner, which is a related sentiment. The Rybergs were simply acting out what so many other citizens felt. If shopkeepers worry about the loss of business, home owners worry about real estate values. A drunk or dirty Mexican, or one who throws trash on a lawn, can seem to threaten their lives.

Though Salas had stolen nothing and was neither drunk nor unruly, the justice system appeared to condone his harsh treatment. Charges were never filed against Rickey Ryberg, the older brother who had walked away. An internal Border Patrol investigation into the alleged complicity of the Border Patrol guard went nowhere. Randy Ryberg was acquitted of felony assault charges, convicted of a misdemeanor for false imprisonment, and sentenced to a short work-release program. The butcher Zimmerman was acquitted of all charges.

Salas went home to his wife and children in Mexico, but not before finding an attorney to represent him in a civil suit against his tormentors. In 1992, he returned briefly to San Diego to accept a cash payment from them in federal court. The *Los Angeles Times* ran his picture and a report under the headline SETTLEMENT EASES PAIN OF MIGRANT'S WOUNDED PRIDE. To those who worry that Mexican immigrants will never integrate into the mainstream of U.S. culture, the story seems a fitting response.

Perhaps ten thousand immigrants hide in the countryside of northern San Diego. Those who are most afraid dig "spider holes" high on the hills, where their enemies cannot get at them without being seen. The spider holes are trenches scooped in the dirt, covered with branches and sheets of plastic, with room perhaps for several men to stretch out. Migrants live furtively in them for months at a time, venturing out to buy food and search for day work. They fear the Border Patrol and police, and also the bandits who roam the brush between subdivisions. Having been paid in cash, they have to save their money and ultimately get it to a post office. If they are among friends, they can work by rotation, leaving someone behind to guard the spider hole. If they are among strangers, they must carry the money and defend it.

Thousands choose safety in numbers and live openly in the squatters' camps, dense clusters of scraped-together shelters reminiscent of the shantytowns south of the border, though more primitive. The squatters' camps have existed in San Diego for at least a century. I know of twin brothers, now eighty years old, who have lived in them since they were fifteen. Although the settlements were always illegal, they were tolerated by landowners who needed the laborers and by authorities who understood the need. All that is changing. The other need, to build dormitories for the workers, has met such strong community opposition that advocates for the migrants have practically given up on it. The advocates are left in an odd position: as the city approaches, they have to defend the very squalor they want to alleviate. They fear that soon even the old twins will be forced onto the hillsides and into spider holes.

For now, the twins live in a camp called Los Diablos, which is home to five hundred men and a few women. It lies in a small valley about a mile from the road, at the end of an eroded track. Isolation discourages the vigilantes and robbers who regularly invade other camps. Nonetheless, Los Diablos sometimes comes under attack at night. Because of this, and the drunken knife fights between residents, it has a reputation for violence. I went there one Sunday and found a settlement of plywood huts clustered in a grove of eucalyptus trees. The afternoon was warm. A jet fighter screamed overhead. Dusty men stood under a tree, methodically drinking beer and flattening the cans with a block of wood. A vendor had arrived in an aluminum-paneled truck to sell groceries and chilled Cokes. Children splashed in a stagnant creek, which trickled with overfertilized irrigation runoff. The ground was heavily littered. At a crude outdoor restaurant the proprietress built a cooking fire and played her battery-powered radio to the empty tables. I crossed the creek on a plank and walked through the camp. Hundreds of men lounged there, whiling away a day without work, washing their clothes, and visiting their friends. The camp had grown inward, for shade and protection, and was surprisingly dense. The huts were made of scrounged plywood and sheet metal, with roofs of plastic held down with rocks, boards, and in one case bent bicycle wheels. If a strong wind had blown the place apart, it could have been rebuilt within hours. There was no lack of manpower.

I wanted to know about border crossings. In the common cooking shed, by a fire strewn with eggshells and charred paper plates, I talked to a group of Mixtecs who were drunk on Budweiser. They had a friend who had been struck by a car while crossing the interstate at San Ysidro. "Fucking *Migra*," one said, slurring his words in Spanish. "When they come, what can we do but run?"

Another said, "I crossed alone and I had to fight bandits. They were three and they spoke English. But I know karate and I knocked them down." He was a slight man with a wispy goatee. Sitting on the bench, wavering, he slashed his hand through the air. Karate provides magic answers to the inequalities of life; I did not wonder that a Mixtec would proclaim the power of his bare hands. His friends nodded somberly at me, as if to verify his dreams. Embarrassed, I jotted down the details.

The smallest man there, who was slightly crippled, wore his baseball hat sideways. He told a more credible story. "Last time I came across, there were ten of us at Otay Mesa and we ran into five bandits with guns. They grabbed one of our guys and said they'd kill him unless we gave them our money. But they didn't get mine because I had it hidden in my shoe."

"What about the Border Patrol?"

"They weren't there." He grinned toothlessly and made the others laugh.

He was the camp clown. The men called him "El Comandante" because of his small size. He had a famous fondness for drink and the whores who visit on Friday nights. I suspected he was young. He had lived at Los Diablos for years and had no thought of leaving.

On the other side of the camp, I spoke to a man who had arrived the night before with his two grown daughters. It was the first time for all of them, and they had crossed along the beach. The man said, "We were afraid, but we never saw bandits or the Border Patrol. We got on the trolley, and in the city we met the man who drove us here. Now we'll try to find work." He looked determined. His daughters sat together in the dirt between two huts. They were plump and Indian, bewildered, and too frightened to talk.

Later I met a sober man with a trimmed beard whose name was Jacinto Juarez. He was thirty-six, although he looked a generation older. When I asked him about crossing the border, he seemed surprised that I wanted to know. He said, "It's not hard. The first time, in 1982, the Border Patrol caught me and told me not to come back. But I wanted to work. The second time was okay and since then I've never had a problem."

"How often have you crossed?"

Too often to remember. At first he divided his life evenly between California and Mexico, spending three months at a time in each. Over the years, as inflation (and expectation) took its bite, he found that he had to work longer and could not afford to go home as often. He obtained legal residency in 1987 and began to cross the border openly, but little else changed. When I met him he had been working eleven months straight at the same nursery that had employed him from the start, and where he still earned only the minimum wage. He said, "I *have* to work here. Otherwise I would live on the streets of Mexico. But I have almost abandoned my family." He meant his wife and eight of his ten children. The two oldest sons had just crossed the border illegally and were living in a spider hole above the camp. Juarez ached to bring the others across and dreamed of renting an apartment. "But the cheapest apartments here are five hundred dollars a month. What good is legal residency if you can't afford a place to live? There must be some way for poor people to exist more easily." He was dispirited. He said, "You want to know about crossing the border, but the real problem is what comes afterward. Look around you at this camp. I am no longer young, and I need my family. But is this the home I should give them? Who does the land belong to? Does anyone know how much longer we can stay?"

It was a good question. Cresting the hills in bright and even rows, new houses march toward Los Diablos. The land on which the camp stands was recently bought by an East Coast investor, whose attorneys worry about his liability. Local government has applied additional pressures because of code violations and poor sanitation. But the investor is sympathetic: he does not intend to develop the land for several years and is willing to let the squatters stay on until then. Migrant activists have quieted the city by renting dumpsters, piping in potable water, and building a communal toilet. To pay the water bill, a collection is taken every month. The money is not easy to extract. Men come and go, and no one is in charge.

Their selfishness has surprised some of the college students who volunteer to teach English at the camp on the weekends. Fooled at first by the shared meals and the ideal of a common humanity, the students eventually learn what the migrants know perfectly well—that any real sense of community is undercut by such brutal living conditions. Poor and uneducated Mexicans are as likely to turn against each other as to band together. They fornicate, lie, and drink. They do not concentrate on lessons, or learn much English, or seem to care that they should. They chop up the benches of the open-air classroom and use the wood to cook their meat. It's very disappointing.

Most volunteers give up. Even the man who had organized the English lessons seemed disillusioned. He was a ruddy thirty-year-old, a professional guitarist and singer of Irish folk songs. He said, "There is something absurd about all these college youngsters patronizing grown men."

Until recently, he himself had lived in the camp. I asked why and he answered modestly, "I was trying to keep my costs down." The truth lay deeper: in addition to the English classes, he had organized medical services, built the toilets, brought in the drinking water, helped the migrants with their immigration papers, and warned them about the most abusive employers.

I asked, "And why did you leave?"

He answered, "There was a killing. And the living was hard. I had stomach problems. Finally, I realized how little I have in common with men who will walk a hundred miles down a railroad track to get to where they're going."

Four

The airplane is no bigger than a car, and it requires no roads. You take off from San Diego, climb through the overcast, and at two thousand feet, with your wing down, you slice into the clear sky and turn east along the border. It is a primeval morning. San Diego and Tijuana have vanished. The stratus below forms a white sea that laps against the mountains ahead. Where the clouds dissolve, you fly across rugged uplands rising to four thousand feet.

Taller mountains stand to the north and south. The desert is brown and scruffy: jeep tracks mar the surface, and abandoned mines spew tailings down the stony slopes. A few ranch compounds nestle by wells in the shade of planted trees. Like opposing images, two highways swing up to the border, turn, and swing away. A railroad in the United States winds through the badlands, ducks through a tunnel, and emerges into Mexico; the rails are rusted and do not glint when you pass overhead. Farther east the ground slopes down into a vast, elongated depression. You descend with it into an intensifying desert until the altimeter reads less than zero and you are flying below sea level. Suddenly the desert vanishes, replaced by miles of crops. The green is shocking. It is an engineered color, a bit too bright, manufactured with artificial rainfall pumped from man-made streams. The water comes from the Colorado River, which flows by just over the eastern horizon.

On the U.S. side this fertile lowland is known as the Imperial Valley. Five hundred thousand acres are irrigated. The fields are large and flawless, and the population is thin. In the winter, retirees from the Midwest fill the trailer parks. They are known with tentative affection as snowbirds. The Mexican side, called the Mexicali Valley, is about the same size but more densely populated. Half the land is held by *ejidos,* communal farms established throughout Mexico during the land reforms that followed the revolution. Until recently, *ejidos* operated under a set of laws that forbade the sale or breaking up of the land. For decades, they provided the government with its strongest claim to a populist legacy. In reality, however, they have long been unloved by the political elites, and even in the fertile Mexicali Valley, they have rarely produced well. Many *ejidatarios,* with rights to work the land, have fled to find work in the United States. The future is represented by the other half of the Mexicali Valley, private farms and small towns bursting with landless workers. There is one city, also named Mexicali, where a million people crowd against the boundary fence. A century ago it did not exist. Now it is the state capital and an important industrial center. In its shadow on the U.S. side lies Calexico, a gritty town of sixteen thousand. There is something temporary and unstable about these places. Like the farms, they live by the uncertain grace of a troubled river.

Geologically the two valleys are the same—a trough called the Salton, filled by thousands of feet of river sediments. The trough was formed by multiple fractures along the southern extension of the San Andreas Fault. The earth's crust is sliding, pulling apart and thinning, and despite the thick alluvial fill, the surface has sunk below the level of the sea. Seventy miles southeast of the border, where the ocean encroaches, the Gulf of California has formed. The gulf is a young sea, a future Pacific. It is blocked from flooding inland by the delta of the Colorado River. The river flows into the scene, southbound after a 1,300-mile odyssey from the Rockies. It edges the Imperial Valley on high ground, enters the Mexicali at the eastern edge, and pushes into the gulf. Its delta has created a mound like an enormous dike across the mouth of the trough. Topography on such a scale is hard to visualize, and it is particularly unusual here because the river flows toward the south, but the adjacent land descends in the reverse direction, toward the north. In other words, from its high points along the river banks and coast, the Mexicali Valley slopes downhill toward the United States. The land passes through sea level at the border, and drops another 270 feet into the Salton sink. The long final descent below sea level defines the Imperial Valley. The sink is the northwest end of the valley, the trough's low point, and it has no drain.

In prehistoric times the Colorado periodically overflowed its banks, turned from the sea, and filled the sink, laying the sediments that are farmed today. The ancient lake has been called Cahuilla, after the Indians who fished along its shores. It evaporated when the river shifted back to the gulf. The basin was dry when white settlers arrived late in the last century. They pronounced the land too thick to drink and too thin to plow, then made plans to farm it. By 1901 the California Development Company had completed the first big canal and was diverting Colorado water into the new fields. Rather than digging an expensive ditch through high terrain, the engineers chose to ship the water along one of the river's natural overflow channels, the Alamo River, which ran through Mexico before swinging north into the United States. The Colorado was only to glad to cooperate: in 1905 it flooded, breached the headworks of the irrigation canal, and eagerly resumed its ancient course through the valleys, wiping out farms and towns. For two years, the entire Colorado emptied into the sink, filling it to a depth of two hundred feet and creating the Salton Sea. After repeated attempts to redirect the river back to the gulf, the Southern Pacific Railroad, an Imperial landowner, finally succeeded in 1907. Today the Salton is a mildly poisonous place, a quarter-million-acre salt lake tainted by selenium and agricultural chemicals. Scientists who predicted it would evaporate within twenty years did not take into account its replenishment from irrigation runoff. In that sense, the Colorado still flows into it. But there is little danger of another flood.

The Colorado River has so many dams and diversions that by the time it approaches the border it contains barely enough water to meet treaty obligations with Mexico. The last of the flow is diverted into the Mexicali canal system by the Morelos Dam, which straddles the U.S.-Mexico boundary near Yuma, Arizona. Below the dam the river is dry and the delta is dormant. For years the only water that has reached the gulf is a trickle of irrigation runoff. On a geologic scale this may prove to be a hiatus, since the reservoirs upstream are silting up. In the meantime, Imperial farmers say, not a drop goes wasted. What they mean is, not a drop goes unused.

In the town of Imperial, I found a pamphlet that boasted of mild temperatures and abundant sunshine in the winter, the rainy season. Here is the other three fourths of the story: the rest of the year is hell. Though the maximum temperature of 119 degrees has been recorded only four times since 1914, almost every afternoon in the summer gets close. You can cook soup by standing a can in the sun. The crepe soles of your shoes melt on hot pavement. The pavement itself melts. Residents call it dry heat, but *parched* describes it better. The average annual rainfall is under three inches. In 1956 the year's total was 0.016 inch. June is the driest month, in which measurable rain has fallen only twice since 1914: 0.04 inch in 1948 and 0.01 inch in 1980.

Nonetheless, the soil is rich, and thanks to the legendary Imperial Irrigation District, the land is cultivated year-round. Water from the Colorado is diverted at the Imperial Dam and flows eighty-two miles through the All-American Canal. The All-American is a giant ditch two hundred feet wide and twenty feet deep. It was dug in the 1930s to bypass the disastrous Alamo ditches and to silence the Mexicans' revolutionary claims to the water flowing through their territory. The three million acre-feet of river water that the canal delivers annually is roughly one-fourth of the Colorado's total flow. An acre-foot is the volume of water necessary to cover one acre to a depth of one foot, which is the amount an average American family uses in two years. Ninety percent of the All-American water goes to the fields, each acre of which receives, on average, nine acre-feet every year. That is a lot of water, but evaporation and transpiration rates are high, and at least a foot is needed just to flush the soil and keep it from becoming too salty. The price is about $11.50 per acre-foot, which is cheap compared with the $1,000 per acre-foot that some water-starved California cities are now considering paying. As a result, fortunes are wrung from the land. The distribution of this wealth is unequal: of only seven hundred farmers in the entire 500,000-acre valley, seventy-two own more than half the land, and many can afford not to live there. The workers, of whom there are thousands, are first- or second-generation Mexicans, and they are poorly paid. As measured by family income, Imperial is the poorest county in California. Nonetheless, the farmers have made it one of the most productive agricultural areas in the world. The desert is never far from view, a reminder of the consequences if ever the water stopped flowing or became too expensive. You have to admire the gall of the farmers: their biggest crop is alfalfa, a cow food that is notoriously wasteful of water. They farm in hell and thumb their noses at the devil.

At the sprawling headquarters of the Imperial Irrigation District, I talked to an official about the problems across the border in Mexicali. He said, "I'm just amazed that the Mexican farmer has to plant his crops on the basis of water availability. Our farmers plant on the basis of the market. Water is a given."

Water is given and then returned. Because of the slope of the land, some of the Colorado River delivered to Mexico ultimately runs back into the Salton sink. It flows across the border in the Alamo River and another natural channel named the New River, born of the 1905 flood. Like other drains in the two countries, both rivers are sick with farming waste. The New River has the additional misfortune of flowing through the slums and industrial zones of Mexicali City. It has been called the most polluted river in the United States.

Wayne Van Der Graff, the Imperial County supervisor from Calexico, took me to the fence, to the gulch where the New River enters the country. Van Der Graff was a retired border guard, a burly red-faced man with seventeen grandchildren. He drove a big sedan with a strong air conditioner. His wife, a friendly and unassuming woman, sat in the back enjoying his company. Van Der Graff said, "Calexico's tough, you bet. In '82 when Mexico devalued the peso, it just about dried up. Things aren't much better now. The town's so poor that the grocery chains send their substandard food here because they know we'll buy it. Chicken wings for thirty-nine cents a pound. Just the same, our school district has a dropout rate of only 6 percent, the lowest in California. And half of our students are immigrants. What does that tell you about the quality of these people?"

For a retired border guard, he seemed sympathetic. I discovered he had founded an orthopedic clinic that over the years had performed fifty thousand charitable operations on children from Mexico. His wife savored my surprise. She said, "Wayne won the supervisor's election in a district that's 95 percent Hispanic, against a Mexican incumbent."

He had campaigned on a platform of cleaning up the New River. He said, "The Tijuana River's just a stream compared to what we have here." We left his wife in the car and walked along the water's edge. A pungent smell of sewage and chemicals wafted from the surface. The flow was narrow, powerful, swirling with brown foam. Van Der Graff said, "The color depends on what they're spilling over there. The chroming plants and slaughterhouses are the worst, but just about all the industries are contributing. The list of toxins in that water is mind-boggling. Not to mention bacteria and contagious disease. That's untreated sewage you're smelling. You've heard about the cholera outbreaks in Mexico? The health department doesn't want us to do anything that would slow the water. At least now the crap keeps moving."

We walked on. He said, "And it's not just the Mexicans. We get American operations crossing over just to dump their wastes into the river. The latest was a batch of printer's ink."

A tire floated in from Mexico. Van Der Graff was sweating heavily in the heat. He said, "You never know what's coming. We find human corpses. Horses and cows, too." He smiled. "When I was in the Border Patrol we made a sport of counting the condoms. They float in from the whorehouses, you know."

We walked back to his car. I repeated what I had been told in Mexico: "The New River? It's always been understood that you can dump anything into it, and because it flows into the United States, who cares? The attitude has been, let the Americans eat shit."

Van Der Graff winced. "It would make sense to go to the source of the pollution, to clean up Mexicali, but the fact is that's not going to happen. The fact is, we're going to have to clean up on this side of the border. It won't be cheap, but we're going to have to do it."

"How?" I asked.

"We run it through a grate for the biggest debris, then pipe it to a sewage plant, then take it through settling ponds with hyacinths and lilies to get the heavy metals out." He wanted to do the same to the Alamo River.

"When?" I asked.

"That's the problem. There are twenty-three government agencies involved. I've been hearing promises since the Border Patrol first sent me here in 1955. We need to get started and see who shows up to stop us."

The preliminary planning had already been completed. Van Der Graff took me downstream into a canyon wasteland where the treatment plant was to be built. He swept his hand and said, "A beautiful recreation area. We'll have water sports, horseback riding, an amphitheater. People will come to spend the winter. We'll attract the best teachers for our schools." Elsewhere on the border, similar projects have been defeated by population growth in Mexico, but I did not want to doubt Van Der Graff's vision. He was a serious man, doing necessary work. And when water flows in the desert, anything seems possible.

The strangest feature of Mexicali City is the way it is lopped off at the boundary. The fence is chain link, topped by a triangular hat of barbed wire. You can walk along it near the center of the city and look north into the fields of the Imperial Valley. Mexicali does not feel like a border town; it has wide, shaded avenues, elegant neighborhoods, excellent schools, a university, and a shopping mall. Still, it is a third-world city. Things often don't quite work—a telephone, a light switch, an appointment. The poor live in cramped central slums, and in looser shantytowns wedged between the industries on the outskirts. If residents are lucky they work as domestic servants, or toil in sweatshops, or sit on assembly lines in the new American factories. If they are unlucky, they rely on their families, or work the streets. They do not seem resentful, though that could change. The rich drive by, denying the desert in black cars with smoked windows. You feel in such a place that you cannot see, that the contrasts blind you and all the middle ground has been obscured.

In downtown Mexicali, within yards of the fence, a tall, bearded man whose right leg has been amputated stands in the traffic in 110-degree heat. If you went there today, you would find him. He sets a can on the ground and does not move. Others stand nearby—a boy without hands, a man without sight, an Indian mother without medicine for her child. The tall man watches them begging, and beneath his beard his expression never changes. He does not hustle or hope. I walked by him day after day and finally stepped into the traffic to drop a few coins in his can. He said nothing and did not look at me.

There are thousands of Chinese in Mexicali City, descendants of the laborers employed by the Americans to dig the first irrigation ditches. Many of them became small farmers in the Mexicali Valley, only to have their land taken from them and redistributed to the communal *ejidos* during the land reforms of the 1930s. It is a sign of their isolation from Mexican society that even the young continue to speak Chinese as well as Spanish. Deprived of their farms, they have moved successfully into business and now own the Chinese restaurants where, by tradition, the middle-class residents of Mexicali eat lunch. I sat in one such restaurant and talked with an unreformed agronomist about the free market in Mexico. The agronomist was a glum man, maybe fifty-five, weathered at the edges, who had fallen from favor at the federal agricultural office. He worried that I would use his name. He looked around nervously and said, "Mexico is too political—resistance to the new orthodoxy is unwise."

In the Mexicali Valley the new orthodoxy means this: the irrigation districts are turned over to the users; water prices go up; crop supports and food subsidies are eliminated; farmers are encouraged to combine, expand, and plant for the market; commercial banking standards are applied to agricultural loans; eventually even the *ejidos* are privatized. The idea of selling communal land has outraged much of agrarian Mexico, but not the Mexicali Valley. Like most of the north, it admires the U.S. model of undiluted competition.

The agronomist was different. He said, "California

growers are already buying up the best land. They use our soil, use our water, hire a few laborers, and send the crops home. We have been through this before." Then he looked embarrassed and said, "You understand, I have nothing against Americans personally."

I answered delicately, "I have wondered about sovereignty myself."

He continued, "Of course, we have an answer. We say we can compete as equals."

"You don't agree?"

"A few farmers can compete, yes, but only a few. Imperial irrigates with three million acre-feet a year of high-quality Colorado water. We get one and a half million at Morelos, and in dry years not a bit more. We pump in another 750,000 acre-feet from our wells—water that is so salty it would kill crops if we didn't mix it with the surface supply."

I couldn't summon much sympathy. He had begun to sound greedy. I said, "The fact remains that you have two and a quarter million acre-feet."

He wagged his finger at me. "This tea we're drinking, it's irrigation water too. Our first priority has to be urban use. Look at the size of this city and the industry moving in. The farmers get only 50 percent of the allotment."

I scribbled some calculations on a napkin. "In Imperial they farm the same acreage with two and a half times as much water."

He slipped on a pair of reading glasses and checked the figures. "You see, we need to conserve water, not imitate the United States."

I said, "I noticed alfalfa here, too." I meant on the *ejidos*.

But he was lost in his thoughts. He said, "Now we grow onions, broccoli, carrots, garlic, all the vegetables. Maybe only one crop a year, but enough to live on."

They also grow cotton, lots of it, which is another thirsty crop and cannot be eaten. But I didn't want to quibble.

He said, "Can you imagine what this valley will look like when only the big farmers are left and all they grow is alfalfa? Think of the water use! They will return the valley to desert. I'm old-fashioned because I ask what will become of the people." He broke open his fortune cookie and chewed it miserably; then he ate mine.

One evening, I went to see an old friend of his, a retired farmer who didn't care about politics but wanted to talk water. I recognized his passion from other desert people. We sat in a gold-carpeted living room, in a middle-class section of Mexicali City. He opened by saying, "It's awful what we've done to the Colorado, very sad. It was once a great river." This, of course, is something everyone can agree on. He plunged ahead: "Do you know, I believe in water witches?" He grabbed an imaginary forked stick and slowly lowered it to the floor. "These people are natural geologists. I've watched them work in Ensenada. The wells there never run dry, no matter how much you pump."

Speaking of miracles, he said, "Once near La Paz I watched goats drinking from the sea! Fresh water!" His eyebrows twitched. "I read in the *Reader's Digest* about people in a raft who were dying of thirst, and drank from the ocean, and found—again, fresh water!" He peered at me. "What do you think of that?"

"Which ocean?"

He did not answer. For twelve years he had farmed in Veracruz, along the rainy Gulf of Campeche. He said, "On the sixteenth of September, 1951, it rained three feet in a single night!"

His memory for dates impressed me. I questioned his measure of the rain.

He said, "Too much rain? I saw the Papaloapan River flooding, three kilometers from shore to shore. It formed a green highway into the sea." He waited expectantly for me to write this down.

I tilted my pad away from him.

He continued, "On the day I came to Mexicali—the thirteenth of July, 1956—two thousand farmers marched in the streets asking for more water." He shook his head in disbelief. "And Veracruz has too much! Can you imagine if somehow we could get it to the northern deserts?"

Similar dreams have drained the Colorado.

To understand the land, keep your eye on the water. After the Morelos Dam, the last of the Colorado flows through Mexico in the main canal called Reforma. The current is too strong and the banks too steep to make swimming safe. But you can fish it, and the water is clear, cool, and beautiful to see. It shimmers in the sunlight and swirls under bridges. It gurgles through gates. It divides, and divides again, until, after fifty miles and perhaps a day, it gushes into the onion fields of Oscar Sanchez Lopez. Sanchez is a university-trained farmer, tall, bald, and thirty-eight. He harvests the onions, crates them up, and ships them north to California. In this form, repackaged, the Colorado comes to Seattle, Chicago, and New York. We eat it with hamburgers raised on alfalfa.

The farm lies close to the riverbed, on the best earth in the Mexicali Valley. To find it, I wandered the back roads through lush, green bottomland. In the distance, past a long blue mirage, the mountainous spine of Baja stretched to the south. Twice I came upon the dunes of the Sonoran Desert, the eastern limit of irrigation, and I turned back. In my enthusiasm for the farms I found landscapes reminiscent of Wisconsin. Then I rounded an unexpected curve and suddenly found Mexico again—a rough-looking town of wood and adobe, with rutted streets and thousands of unemployed. Known simply as Kilometer Fifty-Seven, the town is famous for its cantinas. The state line between Baja and Sonora splits it, as does the change in time zones. On New Year's Eve, while all Mexico celebrates midnight with dancing and gunfire, Kilometer Fifty-Seven celebrates it twice. That is its claim to glory.

I drove up to a young man pushing a flavored ice cart and asked in Spanish for directions to the Colorado. He said, "Colorado?"

"The river, Colorado."

He answered just to answer, "Oh, the river, yes, the river," and directed me east, which I knew already was the wrong direction. He wanted to be helpful. I thought maybe he didn't think of the Colorado as a river. I drove west, and found it outside of town—a mile-wide braid of dry sand and salt cedar. Once it must have been a sight in a flood.

Oscar Sanchez was waiting for me when I pulled up to the farm. He did not make me feel foolish for wandering, but commented on the lack of good maps. I thought he looked and acted more like a diplomat than a farmer. He dressed neatly, carried a calculator in his shirt pocket, drove a LandCruiser, and spoke flawless English. He told me he had spent a year as an exchange student in White Lake, South Dakota. "Nice folks," he said and answered his car phone. It was his wife, calling from their house in a middle-class district of Mexicali City, an hour's commute away.

I asked about his wife. He said she was born in California and raised in Calexico. She had retained her U.S. citizenship. He talked about their two young children. I asked him frankly if he didn't feel they should be educated in the United States. He said, "My wife went to school in California until high school, then got to Mexico and found she was behind in every subject. They let her pick her curriculum in the United States. She didn't learn much."

Sanchez, who was educated in the Mexicali schools, had the mirror experience. "For us, calculus and trigonometry were required subjects. When I got to South Dakota, they weren't even offered." Nonetheless, he had learned in other ways from the United States. As a child he had traveled the roads of Imperial with his father, observing the techniques of American farmers, stopping to measure the crops, or finger the soil. His father was director of the Mexican irrigation district, a farmer himself, and an agricultural historian. The family was comfortable but not wealthy. Of the six children, Oscar alone took an interest in farming. Every Saturday he went with his father to the family farm, at first to play and later to tend some cows. While studying agronomy at the university in Mexicali, he grew his first big crop—of broom corn. After graduating he went to work for the government as a technical adviser to the communal *ejidos* of Ensenada. The experience frustrated him. He told me about a project to find the best location to place a cooler for storing potato seed. "We spent a full month evaluating the sites. Finally the *ejidatarios* put the cooler wherever they wanted."

I said, "A full month seems like a long time."

He shrugged. "Another problem with the job."

Sanchez quit the government in 1986 and went to work on the farm. Now, in the heat of a May morning, he took me for a tour. By Imperial standards it is a small operation: two hundred acres of well-drained soil, ten full-time employees, nine tractors, three disks, two plows, two chisels, two cultivators, three planters, two sprayers, three pumps, and six hundred acres' worth of irrigation piping. During the peak of the winter harvest, four hundred laborers come to pick the crops and to clean, sort, and pack them. The day I arrived, about two hundred were at work in the fields and the packing plant. Last year the farm produced 10,000 boxes of squash, 10,000 boxes of peppers, 20,000 boxes of radishes, 70,000 boxes of zucchini, and 200,000 boxes of green onions—all sold to the United States.

Surprised by the quantities, I asked, "Who eats green onions?"

He said, "This year there are ten million boxes of green onions on the market. There are forty-eight bunches to a box. There are seven onions to a bunch. So everybody eats green onions. Americans eat the white side. Japanese go for the green side. They eat onions backward."

He showed me the office, a roofless two-story building

of yellow brick, which he called "a monument to remind me not to start things I don't have the money for." Then he drove me through the fields. There were eleven, numbered on the farm's computer according to the sequence of the water flow. Sanchez referred to them by their original names, El Mesquite, Las Palmas, El Puente, Pedro, and El Ocho, which is number eleven on the computer.

Sanchez said he would like to double his acreage, but only if it can be done efficiently, for instance by acquiring his neighbor's sesame fields. We walked over to see them and Sanchez said, "If you want a crash course in agriculture, here's what not to do." I took his word for it: his own fields were much prettier. I mentioned the farmers in the Midwest who take pains to plant evenly, and who care about matching the colors of their farm equipment. He admitted the aesthetics mattered to him, too. "You can be a salesman and not love your work. But a farmer?"

We drove to the north side of the farm and watched a contract crew using a laser surveying device to level forty acres. Level fields conserve water and produce uniform, unblemished crops. Uniformity and beauty is important in the U.S. market—wholesalers and consumers demand it. Sanchez has managed to meet the strict standards of his buyer in California. Nonetheless, his boxes are stamped MEXICAN, and worth less for it. He brought it up, then told me, unconvincingly, that he didn't care.

I asked why he sold exclusively to the United States.

"Because in Mexico there are always problems collecting. With the United States, business can be done over the telephone. You set a price; they send you a check."

Sanchez can grow crops year-round only because he

rents water rights from less energetic landowners; he worries constantly about his supply. He asked me, "Did you read *Time* on the Colorado—how even after the drought ends there will not be enough to go around?"

"But there's a treaty. You'll always receive your one and a half million."

"I don't trust the treaty if the drought continues."

Even within the treaty he has had problems with the delivery of water. He blamed the inefficiency and arrogance of the Mexicali Irrigation District, where his father still had an office. He said, "Last year we were doing a thousand boxes of zucchini a day, until suddenly they cut our water. Our production dropped to four hundred."

We went to a freshly planted onion field and watched water cascading from rows of sprinklers. Sanchez squinted with an artist's eye and spoke about the wet reflection of light on the surface: "We'll water until the mirror is uniform."

The sprinklers were driven by a roaring diesel pump, drawing four hundred gallons a minute from a ditch. A muddy, bare-chested man stood next to it clearing the intake. He watched us warily. Sanchez called him a loner, the pump man, the farm's most important worker. He had the dedication of a ship's engineer. Through the worst summer heat he tended the pump unceasingly, eating and sleeping beside it. I asked how much he made. Sanchez poked at his calculator and came up with twenty-three dollars a day.

Other workers make one-fourth that. We came upon a large crew picking onions. Speaking of the workers, Sanchez said, "Every one of these will go to the United States. They don't think of going to school, only of emigrating.

They still think they can sweep money off the streets there." In the meantime, whole families stooped in the fields under a blazing sun. The girls wore long sleeves and covered their faces with bandannas to keep their complexions from turning dark. Grandparents huddled in the shade of draped sheets, caring for the youngest children. Infants slept in field boxes.

Sanchez had a quick talk with the foreman. The workers spoke to him as they passed. Relations seemed friendly and informal. I wandered through the field to where a group of men and women sat, sorting and tying the onions with deft motions, chattering all the while. Sanchez caught up with me and said, "We pay them by the box. The fastest people can make fifteen dollars a day. Tying onions becomes so automatic they can gossip while they work." He grinned. "They say the worst things you can imagine, like about my cousins."

"What about them?"

"That they're homosexuals."

"And what do they say about you?"

He grinned again. "That's easy. They think farmers are the luckiest men in the world. They tell each other I live in a castle. They think I have all the money."

Which he did, of course, compared to them. As do the American consumers. The line from the fields to the grocery stores runs short and straight. Within three days, these onions would be on those shelves, priced to sell.

I wanted to carry the conversation to its end. I said, "The workers are poor, but they're probably healthy."

Sanchez didn't go for it. He shrugged doubtfully and said, "Yeah, but they look a lot older than they are."

But there were limits to his sympathy, as there are

limits to ours. The farm is flanked by a main canal, which runs next to train tracks and the paved highway to town. Along its length, squatters have built shacks and planted vegetable gardens, which they irrigate illegally by siphoning water. Many have tapped into the power lines, and recently some have installed television antennas. Such squatters are a common feature along all the Mexicali canals. I asked Sanchez what he thought of them.

He said, "Do they bother me? You bet they do. Not for the money, but for the water they steal."

"Water is money," I said.

He corrected me with the first rule of the desert: "Water is life."

I asked what he did about the squatters at the farm.

"We pull the siphons when we're irrigating, when we have time, but you have to realize this is Mexico and the squatters have rights." He smiled unhappily. "People's rights. Since the revolution we've come to expect it. We think it's normal."

I said, "I'm not sure 'people's rights' are all bad. I met a woman in Mexicali who said the only reason she had hope is that Mexico still has heart."

Sanchez was unimpressed. "Yes, of course. But look, after the revolution all the laws were against capitalists—as if the workers and farmers aren't capitalists, too! Now the system has failed and we can no longer afford it. We see the former communist countries changing because the system didn't work there either. This is something we've got to confront. The time has come, and not just because the Americans say so."

We visited a neighboring *ejido,* one of the communal

farms that the government would like to do away with. It was a dormant village of a thousand people, with an overgrown playground and several thousand acres of neglected fields. Sanchez looked grim. He said, "This is good land, the best! It's a disgrace. Since the land belongs to no one, no one cares."

It was not entirely true. We went into Kilometer Fifty-Seven and met an *ejidatario* who still did care. Antonio Vargas was an aging and gnarled peasant in a straw hat. He had done business with Sanchez, and the two men had become friends. The three of us sat together in a fly-infested cafe that smelled of tortillas and lard. Vargas did the talking. In 1946 he had fled the poverty of Michoacan and had come north to Mexicali to work on his uncle's farm. He counted himself lucky: soon afterward, the *ejido* was formed on land expropriated from an American company and he was awarded fifty-five acres to cultivate. Standard *ejidal* restrictions applied: Vargas could cultivate the land and leave it to his children, but he could neither sell it nor rent it out. For decades this was as basic to the makeup of Mexico as its centralized, national industries or the protectionism of its trade policies. Now in his old age, Vargas felt the world shifting under him. It made him angry.

I said, "But the *ejido* has failed, hasn't it?"

He didn't want to admit it. He said, "The land is excellent. Somehow we make it through. It gets to the point where there are too many in the family for the land, so people have to emigrate. That's not the fault of the *ejido*. From my village in Michoacan, half the people have moved to the United States."

I insisted. "Still, something's wrong with the *ejido*. I've seen the abandoned fields."

"It's the government's fault. They always decided how much money would be lent for which crops. They would say, 'This year we want six million acres of wheat.' And they would make us plant wheat. Then they would buy the wheat. The prices were always adjusted so the farmer wouldn't make money."

"What kept you from raising a different crop or selling to a different buyer?"

He nodded heavily. "I tried. I even raised grapes. And I always tried to sell the wheat to anyone beside the government. I sold some last June and I still haven't been paid."

I asked about the idea of allowing the sale of the land. He answered, "First they eliminated the *ejidal* loans. Now they want us to go to the commercial banks. They know we can't afford the interest—we have good land, but not enough. It's all part of a plan. They want to take the land from us. They force us into debt, then allow us to sell. I don't care about myself, but what about my son? And what about his son?"

"What should be done?"

"The government should protect the price of our crops."

After Vargas left the café, Sanchez said, "He blames the government, then turns to it for solutions. He's a good man, but like all of them he's been living too long on subsidies."

I said, "He looks south. Did you notice that he never mentioned the American market? You look north. Are you so sure it's the right direction?"

"I should be afraid of the changes, too. The big American corporations are coming in here, forming partnerships and buying up land. They'll run me out of business if I'm not careful. So I'm having to think. Already, I'm experimenting with exotic crops that are too small for the factory farms and where cheap labor will allow me to stay competitive. I'm looking at the ethnic markets. Did you know that Vietnamese eat more jalapeños than we do?"

Speaking of the free market reforms, thinking of reaction, I asked, "You're not worried about the shock to the Mexican system?"

He sidestepped the question. "Sometimes you know what's going wrong, but you can do nothing about it. And then sometimes you just have to change. At any price."

Five

Having outlawed drugs, we now have more reason to fear them. In southern Arizona, I counted ten federal agencies trying to distinguish drug smugglers from ordinary citizens. They use linked computers, data bases, and all the power of the law. They are helped by city police, county sheriffs, and state troopers. At the ports of entry national guardsmen search vehicles. In remote deserts the regular army conducts training exercises designed in part to intimidate. The Corps of Engineers carves access roads; the air force, navy, coast guard, and marines all contribute when they can. In El Paso the Pentagon's Joint Task Force Six treads a fine line of involvement in civil affairs, distributing military hardware and advice to police forces. Nonetheless, the drugs keep coming. Florida is an old story: nationwide, almost all the marijuana, half the cocaine, and a third of the heroin are now smuggled in from Mexico. No one knows how much gets through, but it amounts to enough for millions of Americans. According to the

National Institute on Drug Abuse, about 13 percent of Americans use illegal drugs, a number that remains constant year to year. Even the most hard-nosed drug warriors admit that demand draws the illegal traffic, and only lack of demand or legalization will stop it. In the meantime, they have orders to fight the problem at the border.

From the White House to the most isolated government outpost, officials quietly admit that interdiction has failed, but the war has assumed a life of its own, and it continues to grow. Officially, the federal government now allots about twelve billion dollars annually to fight drugs, 70 percent of which goes to law enforcement. The real expenditure is higher, hidden in more obscure budgets and intentions. I was told that one Border Patrol chief had recently ordered his agents not to worry anymore about catching aliens, to go out and catch drug runners. The man needed to produce drug seizures to please Washington. The search for progress is the guiding principle of endless battle: in Vietnam we counted corpses; here we count pounds. Big seizures are rare, and the agencies squabble incessantly over money and reputations. In the desert their trackers track one another. A coordinating effort called Operation Alliance only highlights the problem it cannot solve. Were it not for a bookkeeping system that allows everyone involved to claim simultaneous credit for seizures, the competing agencies might resort to sabotage.

The bookkeeping system generates "attaboy letters" for the agents of the air division of the U.S. Customs Service. In Tucson I talked to a pilot who had just received his first one. He laughed and said, "I was three hundred miles away, but I happened to be in the air when someone got busted." After four more letters, he said, he would get an ace patch for his flight suit. I presumed he meant his blue jeans—like most of the pilots, he looked a little street-worn. He said he wasn't holding his breath waiting for the next bust: in three years with Customs Air he had not yet seen action. That is one problem with the job. To the extent that your efforts succeed, you won't find many airplanes to chase.

Air-traffic-control radar is designed to follow legitimate flights, not to detect low-altitude intruders. Until recently a smuggler willing to fly a few hundred feet off the ground could come across the Mexican border unseen. Customs relied on a loose network of informants to call in suspicious airplanes. It did not work. When I lived on the ranch near Marfa, Texas, I sometimes heard the smugglers come over at night, flying blacked-out airplanes. I remember the distinctive rumble of a DC-3, and its silhouette cruising the valley through the light of a full moon. My job as an air-taxi pilot gave me opportunities to fly low and occasionally to cross the border illegally without a flight plan. Never once was I questioned. But today the flying is not so easy, since Customs has erected an electronic fence the length of the border.

The fence takes the form of six tethered balloons carrying military surveillance radars. The balloons, which float ten thousand feet above the surface, are called aerostats. The term sounds impressive but lacks precision. All balloons—whether hot air or helium, Zeppelins or toys—are aerostats: they fly not by dynamic lift, achieved by forcing air down, but by static lift, which is analogous to a ship's floating. Roughly the size of a Boeing 747, the Customs balloons look like puffy white blimps with bulbous radar pods and oversized tailfins. They hold fixed positions at the end of Kevlar umbilical cords. In desert sunlight they shine brilliantly; at night they flash with powerful strobes to keep airplanes away. The idea is not a new one: tethered balloons were used for reconnaissance during the U.S. Civil War, and they were widely deployed along the Western Front during the First World War. They were called "captive balloons" in English, and *Fesselballone* in German— *Fessel* being "fetters." They carried artillery spotters, who telephoned their observations along wires built into the tethers. When attacked by fighters, the spotters had to jump; this was the first regular use of parachutes.

The Customs balloons are different in one important way: they carry radar instead of man. The radars do not blink, jump, or worry about their girlfriends. From the maximum altitude 10,000 feet above the surface, they sweep the horizon for 150 miles around. Combined, they form an overlapping polka-dot line from the Pacific to the Gulf of Mexico. The balloons are tethered in Yuma and Fort Huachuca, Arizona; in Deming, New Mexico; and in Marfa, Eagle Pass, and Rio Grande City, Texas. Their gleanings are transmitted to the Customs radar room in Riverside, California, east of Los Angeles.

The system is not invincible. Already four balloons have crashed and been replaced. They are vulnerable to, among other things, high winds, dust devils, jet stream turbulence, standing waves, ice, and snow. Thunderstorms, which hit the border by the thousands, are their mortal enemies.

In Fort Huachuca, I stood with a ground-crew chief while he eyed a growing thunderstorm and ordered his ship reeled in. He was a retired fighter pilot with a chiseled jaw. He gave me his plan for weather. "If the cell's ten miles out, we'll fly at ten thousand. Cut the distance in half, and we're down to five thousand. The idea is to dock it, secure it"—he pointed to the pavement—"and step across that yellow line when the first drop falls. If the crew gets wet, I buy steaks." It seemed like a reasonable plan, because the balloon was fairly safe when secured to its docking mast; but it meant that the balloon spent much of its time on the ground, where the radar is essentially blind.

There is another problem. A balloon is like a giant flag—when you raise it, you proclaim your seriousness; by hauling it down, you signal that the border is again open for business. In theory, Customs can fill the gap by sending in one of its long-range patrol airplanes. The patrol airplane is the Lockheed P-3, a four-engine turboprop shouldering an early-warning radar—fancy battlefield hardware, expensive to buy and to fly. Customs has four based in Corpus Christi, Texas. It uses them mostly offshore to watch deep into Mexico and Central and South America. This means that when the balloons are hauled down, as they are regularly, the chances are that no patrol airplane is available. With equipment like P-3s, you don't sit around waiting for bad weather in Fort Huachuca.

The Customs agents are not naive about their task. They have flown the border for decades, and know its size and emptiness. From altitude over southern Arizona, the view is so vast that the cities look like cloud shadows and the mountains like veins under the skin of the earth. This is hot drug-running country, on the direct line to California. Customs never claimed that it could stop the air traffic, only that it could slow it. And despite the problems with the radar fence, the effort appears to be succeeding. The goal of a one-in-four interdiction rate no longer seems impossible.

Interdiction means more than seeing your quarry on radar—you have to catch it, too. That is where the aircrews come in. Once a suspicious airplane has been spotted, they fly out to intercept it, follow it, and seize the load. Aircrews are positioned at airports all along the border. The Tucson station, at Davis-Monthan Air Force Base, is one of the biggest, and it is first in numbers: in one recent year it generated 170 arrests, 18 seized aircraft, 140 seized cars, 6,000 pounds of cocaine, 26,000 pounds of marijuana, $5 million in cash, and untold attaboy letters. There is new drug-fighting money here, and lots of it. Since 1985 the staff has grown from fifteen to ninety, half of whom are pilots. Their main interceptors are $8 million versions of the Cessna Citation business jet, equipped with F-16 target radars and forward-looking infrared scopes. The Citation is a match for the opposition: it can dash to 400 miles an hour and slow to 100, climb to 40,000 feet or hug the surface. It cannot, however, operate out of the short dirt runways preferred by smugglers. For the final stage of the chase Tucson sends out the Sikorsky Blackhawks, powerful $16 million military helicopters equipped with night-vision devices. The Blackhawks carry the "bust crews," meaning anyone who happens to be sitting around the station. Everyone wants to go. Sometimes there is gunplay, but the agents don't think of the dangers. Busts break the monotony of the job.

Between flights the crews endure a firehouse routine. They thumb magazines, read technical manuals, and hope for a call. They don't talk much, because they have said it before. They watch videos. They run missions to Burger King. On some shifts they practice emergency procedures, or fly off in one of the confiscated airplanes and poke around the border airports. Sometimes they get calls from the police for their Boelkow helicopter with the forty-million-candlepower "night sun" spotlight that can blind a football stadium. "Very psychological," one pilot told me. "It intimidates people."

When the weather is good, the jet crew is expected to take a Citation out and cruise the border for a few hours, searching for traffic with the F-16 radar. They call it trolling; it's a way of keeping their flight hours up and practicing their intercepts. To avoid a pattern, they fly where they want, when they want.

The crew I accompanied chose southeast Arizona, where the Fort Huachuca balloon had been hauled down again. We climbed on autopilot past blossoming clouds to seventeen thousand feet. The captain, named Sayrahder, had long blond hair and a lean, aging face. His copilot looked like a plump fraternity boy; his name was Cruciger, but they called him Junior. It was his turn to fly the airplane.

The only action around was one of their own Black-hawks coming at us, trundling east to El Paso at 150 miles an hour. We picked it up on the target radar, nine thousand feet below. Sayrahder radioed the other pilots and

Cruciger showed me his technique—a cold, stern intercept. He turned toward the helicopter, passed it high and fast, dropped behind into its blind six o'clock position, slowed, and crept up until he locked into place about twenty feet behind it and slightly to the side. The idea is to read the registration number on the tail, transmit it to Riverside, and then, if the computers do not suspect a smuggler, depart without being seen. Sayrahder thought Cruciger had approached too aggressively, and reminded him of another Customs pilot who had shot past a suspect airplane, unable to slow in time. We watched the Blackhawk's tail vibrate, commented on the shaking of helicopters in general, and accelerated away through a steep turn. Then we came around for a high-speed pass, clipped past the Blackhawk at 400 miles an hour, and swept into a climb. The helicopter pilot radioed his laughter and said, "Whooee, Junior's bad."

We returned to the patrol. I asked the pilots how they decided which targets to intercept. They said, more or less, we use discretion, we don't intercept the airlines. Two hours later we had someone on radar, off to the right, doing 140 miles an hour eastbound at 9,500 feet. Riverside checked the airplane's recent flight path and confirmed that it had been tracking the airway. Cruciger looked eager and Sayrahder said, "Lotta times they'll try to mix into the legitimate traffic." He flew the intercept and approached carefully from miles astern. Standard radar shows an airplane as a symbol on an electronic map; forward-looking infrared radar shows a ghostly image of the target much as you would see it with the naked eye. The airplane ahead began to take on definition in infrared while it was still only a speck in the sky: high wings, two engines, slow-turning propellers, strange outboard pods. Closer in, we discovered it was a flying boat, a Grumman Albatross. Sayrahder snuggled up to the tail and the airplane filled our windshield. Because of the aquatic curvature of the hull, Cruciger had trouble reading the registration number, and Sayrahder had to move farther to the side. This did not please him, because it put us within view of the other cockpit—but, as he said, how often do pilots look back? Once we had the number, we dropped into a trailing position and waited while Riverside ran a check. The check came up empty, as it almost always does. We got a name and address in Miami, no history of smuggling, and we turned away.

The U.S. Customs Service's facility in Riverside, California, is known in government jargon as C^{3}I, or "C-cubed-I," for command, control, communications, and intelligence. It is the home of Customs' knowing eye, the border voyeur. The headquarters building is a tan fortress on March Air Force Base, enclosed by fences and barbed wire, watched over by television cameras. The lobby is an armored room, where a uniformed guard questions visitors through thick glass. But he smiles easily and has grown bored with the precautions.

The building hums with air-conditioning. It is heavily carpeted. The people who work there dress neatly and look like headquarters staff. Before letting me into the radar room, they cleared classified information from the consoles, hinting that it related to politically sensitive joint operations south of the border. Direct U.S. involvement in Mexican counternarcotics operations has increased in recent years, the theory being that an American presence will stiffen the resolve of weak-willed Mexican police forces. The Mexican leadership knows that if its reforms are to succeed, it must move against corruption—perhaps Mexico's most intractable problem. This is one way to do it, or at least, in the eyes of Washington, to *appear* to do it. Sending U.S. forces into Mexico is, however, an extremely delicate policy, as the Drug Enforcement Agency has learned from the killing of its agents. Sending radar beams is much safer.

The enthusiast who demonstrated Riverside's tracking system was a sharp-faced young radar operator who had learned his trade as an officer in the air force. I will keep the list of wonders short: The system can track two thousand targets at a time. It looks deep into Mexico, combining returns from the balloons, air-traffic control, patrol airplanes, and the military. It superimposes those returns on detailed ground maps that show the smallest dirt tracks. It picks up road traffic. It provides names, criminal records, traffic violations, and personal financial reports.

You can sit for hours watching traffic move across the screen. We pulled up information at random from declared flight plans: the names of the pilots, where they lived, where they were going. We didn't bother with their bank accounts. The radar operator was absorbed in his work; he called the tracking system the best video game in town. We talked about ways to fool it. He said: You can slow an airplane to car speeds, stick to a Mexican highway, and then dash across the border. You can fly north in the shadow of a train and at the last moment break off. You can work a piggyback scheme with two airplanes, one declared and one not, flying so closely that they merge on radar. You can cross the border legally, avoiding suspicion with a flight plan, drop the load to a ground crew, and return to Mexico without touching down.

For each of these moves the radar operator had a counter-move.

I said, "You can send the stuff on the airlines. You can also wait for a balloon to go down, then take your chances."

He looked at me with disappointment and answered, "They're organized and they're smart." He meant, the opposition would never be so unimaginative.

He thought of himself as a chess player. But he could not explain the logic of the moves that followed: as we watched, a target flying at 500 miles an hour streaked in from the south and landed on a ranch airstrip just below the Rio Grande, in the state of Coahuila. Like many ranches in northern Mexico that have runways, this one was a known staging ground for drug runners. According to Riverside's maps, the runway there was dirt and barely 3,000 feet long—short for what was clearly a small jet.

The radar operator was delighted. He said, "It's incredible what those pilots can do."

But physics governs flight and there is no magic to performance: shoehorning an airplane takes little extra skill; it requires only that you gamble. And the entire drug business, like any black market, thrives on risk. Risk eliminates small-time bunglers, restricts the competition, and keeps the profits up. The big drug organizations depend on Customs to help them with this.

Now a slower target took off from Del Rio, Texas, crossed the river, and flew into the field where the jet had landed. Riverside alerted a Customs flight crew. After ten minutes on the ground the two suspect airplanes took off from the ranch, turned north, declared themselves to U.S. Customs by radio, and landed back at Del Rio. They were met by hard-charging agents. We got word at Riverside: the jet was a French-made Falcon 10, and the slower airplane was a single-engine Cessna Centurion. Both appeared clean, but the Cessna pilot claimed that he had never seen the jet before. The agents started tearing the airplanes apart.

In Riverside the radar operator called up the performance specifications for the Falcon 10 and discovered that the airplane was missing from the data base. He did get the numbers for larger models, the Falcons 20 and 50. I glanced at the stated runway requirements: they were the most conservative possible figures, the lengths a pilot might calculate at maximum weight with company executives aboard, and they understated the real capabilities of the airplanes. No wonder in the eyes of the government the smugglers seem superhuman—they do not play by the official rules.

I noticed the same tendency in Tucson: on nights when thunderstorms are raging and the balloons are down, the Customs crews are not expected to fly their random patrols. This is as it should be, since thunderstorms are dangerous. But as a result, the weather provides cover for smugglers who fly anyway, picking through the storms, taking risks with the mountains. In a perverse way, this pleases me: there are summer nights when the Arizona sky is still wild.

Del Rio found no drugs on the airplanes. Riverside entered the registration numbers into the suspect list, and I went for a sandwich with some of the agents. They complained about the ability of the smugglers to outmaneuver them and the clumsiness of their own response. They blamed bureaucracy.

I said, but your role by definition is to wait; even your intelligence is merely an attempt to predict your opponents' initiatives.

The assistant chief was not happy with my description. He wanted to use the word *proactive*.

I asked if they felt restrained by the courts and they said sure, but less now than before. The conversation turned to a congressional proposal floated in the 1980s that would have allowed Customs to shoot down suspect airplanes.

A slick-talking man said, "That was crazy. We make one mistake, take out one Mexican doctor with his family in a Bonanza . . ." He shook his head at the thought of the consequences.

A burly helicopter pilot disagreed. "What mistake? You're up there looking in this guy's window and hell, you *see* the dope. And he flips you off. Or he does this . . ." He sucked air and made a show of smoking a joint. "We've even had them drop their pants and moon us. They just laugh and head back to Mexico."

"There's nothing you can do?" I asked disingenuously.

"Not the way it is now."

Still, they had a couple of stories. One pilot raised a smuggler on the radio and said, "Land." The smuggler answered, "No way," and turned toward Mexico. The pilot radioed, "This is a joint operation. There's a Mexican *fede-*

rale on board and his people are waiting on the other side."
So the smuggler landed, was arrested, and said, "Hey, that
wasn't fair—there was no *federale* on board." And the pilot
said, "Fair?"

"Do you mean he was so afraid of the Mexican police?"
The helicopter pilot laughed. "Police, army . . . Unless
you've paid them off, they'll blow you out of your boots."
The slick man said, "Then they'll take your watch."
The next story was shorter: A Customs pilot pumped
two rounds through a smuggler's wing. The smuggler
landed.

Those were the old days, a decade ago, when Customs
Air was underfunded and the pilots were frustrated. Despite their grousing, they no longer are. The slick one
admitted it. "Don't get us wrong. We've finally got the
setup and we're doing the job. Our traffic is down by 60
percent. We're getting better all the time. We feel pretty
good about that."

They feel good because the job is compartmentalized.
Their orders are to take the smugglers out of the air, to
channel the traffic, to put it on the ground. The larger
problem is beyond their control: once you force the smugglers to the ground, they are harder to stop. If they can't
fly the dope, they truck it in or bring it on the backs of
men. There are 400 million crossings of the border every
year, and the future belongs to free trade.

Southwest of Tucson, in an emptiness of jagged ridges
and wild valleys, lies an Indian reservation the size of
Connecticut. For seventy miles it backs on the border,

which is marked by a simple cattle fence. This is the high country of the Sonoran desert, with thick growths of cacti and small-leafed bushes, watered in summer and winter by seasonal rains. The people who live here are the Tohono O'odham, a loose configuration of Pima-speaking Indians also known as the Papago. Like many Indian groups, they are poor and troubled, and survive largely on government handouts.

Their ancestors lived a seminomadic life across large tracts of the desert. When the border intruded, in 1854, slicing their land in two, its immediate effect was to provide a refuge in the United States from persecution in Mexico. While Mexican settlers were pushing the Indians aside in Sonora, across the line in Arizona the O'odham lived in valleys no one wanted and fought alongside the army against their traditional enemies, the Apaches. As "good Indians" they were mostly left alone. The southern O'odham began to migrate north. Since Mexico has never believed in reservations, those who did not flee were slowly absorbed into the mestizo population. By 1900 the identifiable population in Sonora had shrunk to a thousand; today it is estimated at two hundred. The holdouts live in remote villages just south of the border, under threat from encroaching ranchers. In desperation they tear down the new fences built across their pastures. Hired cowboys answer with flashed weapons and mutilated cattle. They call the Indians squatters, and they bulldoze their vacant houses. The Indians say they will fight—brave words in a violent land. This is the backcountry of Sonora, a long way from Mexico City, and justice has been corrupted.

But the holdouts are not alone; the official count underestimates the strength of the O'odham in Mexico. It is based on a legalistic definition of the border and on "pure race" concepts that do not necessarily reflect people's views of themselves. Many O'odham are still seminomadic. They live a few weeks here, a few weeks there, and do not let the border stand in their way. I talked to a tribal official who said that a third of the families on the U.S. reservation retain close ties to Mexico. They keep households in the Mexican villages, shop in Mexican stores, and pray in the Mexican churches. They attend festivals and visit friends. Crossing the border here is illegal, but there are thirteen gates in the cattle fence and they are left open.

I asked a tall young man to name the gates. We stood by a trailer in Sells, Arizona, the capital of the reservation. Speaking softly from the chest, clipping the words with his throat in the Indian way, he said, "Buenos Aires, Newfields, Valenzuela, San Miguel, Whitehouse, Vamori, Itak, Rockpoint, Serapo, Christmas, Papago Farms, Salt Well, Menenger's Dam. There's a bunch of cuts in the fence ain't got a name."

He had done a stint in the U.S. Navy as a jet mechanic, and now lived in Mexico, helping his grandmother with her cows. Since his truck had broken down, he was spending a few days in Sells. I asked, "Are you a Mexican or U.S. citizen?"

He looked away at the mountains. "What do you mean?"

"What passport do you have?"

"Don't have one."

"If you had one."

He pulled out his wallet and showed me his tribal card. "Tohono O'odham. The O'odham Nation."

Later he told me he had been a heavy drinker. "But

three ghosts came, told me I'd have trouble. So I don't drink no more and I don't do dope." I asked him if he ever had done dope. He did not answer. I told him I had come to write about smuggling on the reservation. It is pervasive and may now constitute the most common occupation among the O'odham. I had heard an O'odham schoolteacher say this is not all bad: success of any kind is better than the hopelessness of the government dole. The argument is a measure of the reservation's despair, and is, of course, repeated in cities throughout the United States. I thought the young man in Sells might sympathize with the smugglers. I said, "I can understand why someone would turn to smuggling."

In his soft voice he answered, "Shoot the bastards."

I mistook his emotion for the zeal of a reformed drinker. "There's a lot of drug use?"

There is, but it was not what he had meant. He said, "All they think about now is the money. Money is not the O'odham way. It's another white man's lie."

The Customs agent responsible for fighting smugglers on the reservation is a lanky white man who does not lie or even shade the truth. His name is Floyd Lacewell: age forty-seven, boots, jeans, turquoise shirt, baseball cap clamped over greying hair, hails from Ajo, Arizona, with a pistol on his hip. One day he said to me, "After fifteen years of the same shit, you look back and wonder what you've done." He smiled wryly, crinkling the leathery skin around his eyes. "The last few years we've caught a bunch, which means there's just a whole bunch more getting through." In other words, while Washington peddles the possibility of wearing down the drug cartels, Lacewell is out in the field getting overrun. About the headquarters staff he said, "And now they walk around carrying two briefcases!" About his own work he said, "It's a civilian version of Vietnam. That makes it the second losing war I've fought." This too made him smile. Frustration has developed in him a sense of the absurd.

The public affairs office loves him anyway, because he has a lean cowboy quality that translates into good television. Even better, of the twenty men who work for him, fifteen are Indian patrol officers, aboriginal trackers whose job is to read the desert for signs of passage. The image-makers hustle up television crews to tape Indians riding horses. For full impact, real Washington-style power projection, a Blackhawk helicopter is sent in to hover in the background and rush forward aggressively. The downwash blows away the signs. Lacewell stands aside and observes the scene contemptuously. He talks about the time a horse threw an Indian during one of these exercises. The officer lay on his back, collecting his dignity. A public affairs staffer ran toward him, instinctively yelling, "Call 911!"

Lacewell lives as far away from Washington as he can get, and he plans to stay away after he retires. His chosen home, Ajo, is a decrepit town just off the reservation, thirty-eight miles north of Sonoyta, Mexico. It stands in the desert at the foot of the Growler Mountains, bordered on the north by the Barry M. Goldwater Bombing Range. At the edge of the abandoned open-pit copper mine there, I spoke to an old miner who described the giant electric shovel standing a thousand feet below us. He said, "It's got one coat of rust on it, that's all. Ready to go. Hardest thing on a shovel is chipmunks eating the insulation."

"Sounds like you think the operation's going to start up again."

"Oh, it'll happen." He lowered his voice. "They say the Japs are interested. They've been sending their people around."

He meant the occasional tourist. At the rooming house where I stayed, a Japanese family arrived one evening, misdirected by a bed and breakfast guidebook. Politely surprised by their surroundings, they retreated the next morning. I do not think they visited the mine.

When I mentioned the old man's theories to Lacewell, he said dryly, "Sure, the Japs already bought the mine. Everyone knows it but them."

Lacewell's wife is half Japanese and can pass for an Indian in Ajo. She writes children's stories. She and Lacewell have two sons, eight and thirteen, and a fourteen-year-old daughter who won the barrel-racing event in the All-Indian Junior Rodeo. Lacewell works out of a confiscated trailer house next to the Ajo jail. He is responsible for 140 miles of border, from the obscure twin villages called Sasabe, west along the O'odham reservation, through the Organ Pipe Cactus National Monument, and finally the Cabeza Prieta Wildlife Refuge. It is a big territory for twenty men to cover, but outside the reservation it is practically uninhabited. Lacewell would find a small airplane practical; instead he has a Ford Bronco. He used my visit as an excuse to get away from the office and drove me south through a desert of saguaro cacti to the port of entry at Lukeville. On the way, he explained the smuggling.

Most of the cocaine comes right through the ports of entry, concealed in truckloads of vegetables or seafood or anything else that Customs can examine only cursorily because it spoils in the heat. The smugglers guard the load from a distance and don't inform the truckers that they are hauling contraband. It is a good technique, likely to become better as trade between the countries increases.

Marijuana, because of its bulk, is harder to conceal and it goes around the ports. Some cocaine does, too. By pickup truck the most common entry is along the dirt roads of the O'odham reservation; the open gates and historic cross-border traffic make smuggling by the Indians difficult to detect. Drug organizations pay up to $5,000 a load and find plenty of O'odham willing to take the risk. The most intricate procedure calls for "heat vehicles" equipped with radios to lead the loads and scout for trouble.

But the surest method is a string of backpackers walking for days through the desert. The backpackers are Mexicans, who make the trip for perhaps $150, which if they could find a job would be thirty days' wages. The packs are made of sugar sacks roped together and weigh up to a hundred pounds. Increasingly, marijuana and cocaine, and sometimes heroin, are combined in a single trip. Led by a guide, perhaps supplied by caches of water and food, the backpackers walk the loads fifty miles north and hide them near the state highways. Some backpackers return to Mexico, while others go on to find work in the United States. Later someone in a car drives out from Phoenix or Tucson and takes delivery of the drugs. These drivers are sometimes armed.

I asked Lacewell about violence, and he said an O'od-ham officer was murdered near the fence. Another survived an attack by two men with AK-47s. Lacewell himself was sniped at from Mexico. In general, the closer to the boundary you get, or the closer to cocaine, the more likely you are to have trouble. But he did not want to overplay the danger. Most smugglers would rather run than fight. "They are not all bad," he said. "I've never seen a backpacker with a gun."

I had noticed earlier Lacewell's ambivalence toward his opponents. That morning at the Ajo jail, we had gone to see a Mexican, and his Indian wife and daughter. They had been arrested by the Border Patrol for smuggling fifteen pounds of marijuana in a false gas tank. Lacewell's eyes took in the anguished mother and daughter, and the downbeaten father. The man had a history of small-time smuggling. Because of mandatory sentencing, he was certain to spend years in prison. The woman and child were to be released. We returned to the trailer, where Lacewell arranged for the state of Arizona to prosecute. He felt no enthusiasm. He said, "What can you do? You've only got so many holes you can put people into. Eventually you've got to start looking for ways not to put them there."

Lukeville is a port of entry, post office, general store, Chevron franchise, and motel. Most residents are government employees. They live close together in a compound and they quarrel. Lacewell spent a few minutes listening to their woes, then drove me west on a rough dirt track along the cattle fence that marks the boundary. He found a place where the fence had been flattened and a car had been driven across. He said, "We used to bury boards with nails along in here and come out in the morning looking for vehicles. It was like working a trout line. Now with all the legalities, there's no way. The smugglers could sue us." He shook his head. "The job used to be a lot of fun."

We drove slowly north toward Ajo, lurching up a rutted back-country track that Lacewell said was used by smugglers. "It's the damnedest thing. The Mexicans'll take a sedan where we can't get a four-wheel drive." The mountains rose around us. Lacewell talked about the javelina, bighorn sheep, and pronghorn antelope. After all the years, the wilderness still drew him. Several times he had been stranded in it, but because he carried emergency food and water, he had escaped unharmed. He said, "It's rough country," which is cowboy talk for it'll kill you. Ten years ago, on the Fourth of July, twenty-six Salvadorans got lost in this desert. Thirteen died of thirst. Lacewell helped find the survivors. More recently, he found another group of immigrants who had strayed onto the bombing range and were hiding under a big wooden target. "Made sense to me. The marines were bombing." We stopped at an abandoned homestead, poked through a shack, and drove on.

He did not look forward to the office. He said, "Ninety percent of what I do anymore is paperwork. And the computer makes it worse. With electronic mail it's too damned easy for everybody to get to you now. I want you to see this—after a few hours there'll be thirty messages addressed to me. Sometimes I think the computers were a gift from the drug cartels." He drove and brooded. "The latest thing now is every office is supposed to get an intelligence analyst. What the hell's he gonna tell me—that marijuana's green?"

He was still brooding when we walked into the office.

He logged onto the computer and read me the first messages, flicking a key to dismiss each one: "Women in federal law enforcement award nomination." *Flick.* "Ponce, Puerto Rico, all vessels in harbor are suspect." *Flick.* "Jamaican posse in northeast El Paso." *Flick.* "A Colombian national seen in Madrid, arrested in Florida." *Flick.* "Retirement notices." *Flick flick flick.* "Here's one that's actually for me." He read it quickly without comment and flicked. "Another one from New Jersey, a ship in Salem. If I see it, I'll let them know." *Flick.* "Okay, this one ought to be good, here's a 'Threat Analysis' for you: 'There is intelligence in the Southwest that jet skis pose a narcotics threat.' " He swiveled away from the computer and pushed his hat back. "Our government in action. It makes you wonder."

The Border Patrol and Customs are siblings so close that inevitably they fight. I talked to a Customs agent, one of Lacewell's lieutenants, who said, "Border Patrol is a hopeless job. The guys who stay are either really dumb, or they develop an attitude of just doing this, running around in the desert for fun."

The parallels to Customs were so obvious that I had to mention them. I found some polite way. We both were embarrassed.

He shifted slightly. "In Customs, the idealists who come down here hoping to save the country are the ones who get frustrated. They snap. They start beating up on people. They have to leave the service."

As dawn broke one day I met Bob Antone in Sells, and we drove south in a four-wheel-drive truck across the reservation and toward the border gate at Papago Farms. Antone works for Floyd Lacewell; he is one of the Customs Service's O'odham trackers, a burly man of forty with longish black hair. He was dressed in jeans and lug-sole boots. Trackers are also known as sign cutters, because they "cut for sign." "Sign" is evidence of recent passage across the land—a tire track, a footprint, a broken branch. "Cutting" is the action that applies to it, whether searching, finding, or understanding. It is a high art. Antone described his work as "Come out here, cut for sign, maybe jump a load." He is a man of few words.

The land was green with mesquite, dense with desert scrub. We followed a dirt road past a white adobe chapel and a village of traditional houses with walls of spiny ocotillo plastered with mud. Later we came to more typical cinder-block houses of the style built by the government on reservations throughout the West. We eased by a cow. An old Chevy sedan passed, swirling dust. Antone peered at the driver, a woman he knew and suspected of occasional smuggling. He said, "I wonder where she's coming from." To stop her, he would have needed a reason to believe that she had just crossed the border.

A Gila monster waddled across the road. Antone said, "Second one I've seen this year. Last year didn't see any. Haven't seen any rattlesnakes this year. Seen a couple run over on the highway, but not out here on patrol."

We passed Papago Farms, a troubled three-thousand-acre irrigation project. The road grew rougher and dissolved into deep puddles still standing from the previous week's rain. We parked by the open border gate, where the road widened and continued south. I walked across the metal grate of the cattle guard, into Mexico. The day was hot already, and I returned to the United States. Antone told me a story: When Customs tried to stop a pickup carrying a load of marijuana, the driver turned around and raced for this gate. Antone blocked the gate with his truck. The driver went around him and sped right through the fence.

I thought, anyone would have. The fence is three strands of barbed wire strung between wooden posts. The only purpose of the gate is to keep the fence intact. When Antone blocked it, he caused some poor cowboy an hour of cursing in the sun.

All day we followed the primitive dirt roads along the fence line and north through the desert pastures. The radio crackled with police talk. "Twenty-three-fifteen would like you to give him a twenty-one at his forty-two." (Joe wants you to call him at home.)

"Ten-four."

Antone drove at walking speed with his head stuck outside, looking down, checking the dirt for tracks, cutting for sign. He told me more stories: We found fresh tracks and followed them through the desert, an hour, a day, two days. We jumped the smugglers and arrested them. Or, we saw where they had been, but they were too fast for us and got away. Once he said simply, "Last week a guy found five hundred pounds of coke under a tree."

The best place to cut for sign is a loose dirt road smoothed and fluffed by recent rain. If you study the ground against a low sun, the tracks appear luminescent. Any fool can read them. Our conditions were different; the earth was packed, dry, and heavily traveled, and soon the sun was high. We saw hundreds of footprints, mostly old and irrelevant. I found them confusing.

Across one road that afternoon we found a group of fresh footprints. Antone studied them, frowning a little. He walked around them and he crouched. He poked at the soil with the toe of his boot to check the depth and compare for freshness. He went out in the desert to see if the walkers had turned after crossing the road. They had not. He pointed and said, "They're guiding on that mountain." He counted fourteen people and concluded that they were immigrants. I asked how he knew. He explained: They're going for speed, not caution; they have small feet, like Indians from Oaxaca; this one's wearing rubber-tire sandals; these are children; and look, here is a woman in high heels. He said they had crossed that morning, and he showed me the weathering that had just begun to soften the edges, and the bird tracks across the prints from a man's pointed street shoes.

Other immigrants are more careful about crossing the dirt roads. Some walk backward to appear to be heading south. Some attach severed cows' hooves to their feet and some attach horseshoes. One man who left a mysterious indentation at the center of each road turned out to be a pole vaulter.

Smugglers leave a different record. They wear waffle-soled hiking shoes or smooth-bottomed sneakers, and they rest every quarter mile, setting down their heavy packs. They camp and sleep. Caution and craft count for more than speed; otherwise the load could have been sent by truck. Backpackers stick to low ground and the heaviest vegetation. They follow cattle trails but otherwise do not walk in single file. When they come to a road, they disperse and cross it at widely different points, seeking hard and stony soil. They brush out their prints. Some wear carpet on their feet. But once the O'odham trackers are onto them, none of it helps. The trackers are persistent and the slightest disturbance attracts their attention—an over-turned pebble, a bent blade of grass. The best among them can follow a trail across bare rock.

Antone discovered tire marks leading unexpectedly into the desert—a pickup pulling a horse trailer. We followed the marks slowly through the brushland until we came to the place where the truck had backed up and turned around. The ground showed that two horses had been unloaded and two men had mounted up. The horse tracks headed south and returned from an angle. Antone and I followed on foot. He moved with surprising agility for someone his size.

He said, "Probably a couple of cowboys, but I don't know who." After a half hour he said, "See how the tracks spread, like they were out looking for cattle?" Still later he said, "Somebody else was out here too, cutting sign, check-ing the area. Looks like Brian. But I noticed back there the trailer tracks were on top of his."

We came to a rock pile, climbed it, and found two empty Budweiser cans. Antone cut for sign south of the rock pile and found nothing. We followed the horse tracks back to where the trailer had been. As we drove away, Antone mentioned, "It was Arivicio and his man out look-ing for strays. Didn't find any. Brian noticed the tire tracks, found the trailer, went out on foot, ran into Arivicio on the way back. Sometime yesterday."

But no matter how well the Customs trackers read the land, the fact remains that they hardly slow the smugglers. I went south of the border to a meeting of O'odham and Mexican cowboys, who described trucks stacked high with marijuana bales, moving under armed guard to staging areas by the fence. I asked about Customs, and one man said, "Day after day we see the dope going through the gates. Sometimes we see Customs."

The meeting had been called because of an increase in cattle rustling. Eight men gathered under a mesquite tree in Mexico, stirring the dirt with their toes, smoking, and speaking softly, mixing words from three languages. During the long silences, when each man looked away, the desert intruded with buzzing flies and birds chirping in the bushes. The land was pale and hot and smelled faintly of dung. I asked an O'odham rancher from the reservation how many animals he had lost to rustlers. He wore a hat with a turned-down brim that hid his eyes. He answered, "Last year I found about thirty tracks in four miles of fence. Just this week I heard a cow sounding like she was getting pulled by the neck."

"What does a cow sound like when she's getting pulled by the neck?"

"You'd have to know."

"What do the rustlers do with the cows?"

He tilted his head back and glanced pityingly at me. "Some they eat, some they keep. Some they butcher and sell the meat."

Wondering how the loss of thirty cows affected him, I asked the size of his herd. He answered, "Sometimes we have drought and they die out. In a good year we ship quite a few. Hard to say how many are out there. We can't do it like the white man and count each one."

I sensed he knew the number within a calf or two.

The men weren't optimistic about stopping the rustling. One rancher had tried to organize regular patrols along the border fence, but had been dissuaded by threats against his family. Most of the rustlers are known—Mexican cowboys who have gotten involved in the drug business and who profit from the lawlessness of the boundary to steal the occasional cow. To stop the rustling, the men agreed, you would have to stop the drug traffic.

One man, a Mexican who wanted to help, said, "I am convinced that in the state of Sonora nothing can be done about anything. The ranchers and drug traffickers have it under control. The army and police have sold out. And the men in power wouldn't appreciate it if we tried to go over their heads to Mexico City."

I said, "But there are changes, real changes."

"And they will answer you, 'That's Mexico City. It will never get here.' These people are damned serious. They are fighting Mexico City and I think they will win."

An O'odham from a village to the south said, "The traffickers are organized and they are ruthless. You are either with them or against them. The people are afraid. When they hear the trucks coming, they hide in their houses."

One night I sat through a storm and waited for traffic with a Customs tracker named Lambert Cross. Cross was a big man with an easy laugh. We were parked off the road in a four-wheel-drive Suburban, a mile north of the gate at San Miguel. Thunder ripped overhead and lightning slashed the valley around us. Floodwaters had risen in the arroyos, cutting off our return to Sells. Cross was happy. He said that sound travels better after a rain, so you can hear an engine at two miles and a truck crossing a cattle guard at five. In the meantime, since no smugglers would come across until the arroyos subsided, he played me a tape of old-timey music by an O'odham group, the Guachi Fiddlers. We listened to the "Tohono Special Polka," the "Second Time in San Xavier Two-Step," the "Pinto Bean Two-Step," and the "Cababie Polka," which is named after a village. He called it pascola music, a dying tradition, and said his brother-in-law is one of the greats. Cross himself played guitar and sang gospel. He once performed at the Indian National Finals, which is a big rodeo in Albuquerque. At my insistence we listened to a recording of him singing "He's My Lord and My King." Afterward he told me, "Jesus is my salvation."

Cross grew up on a small branch of the reservation along the Gila River. His family had eighteen horses for plowing and pulling wagons. Each night they were turned loose and each morning before breakfast Cross went out to find them. By the age of ten he was an accomplished tracker. The family chopped mesquite, sold the wood, and with the money bought coffee, sugar, salt, bacon, and lard. Everything else they grew or hunted. They were so poor that they bought the children shoes two sizes too big and made them go barefoot when they came home from school. At night they sat by their radio listening to the

Lone Ranger ride with his loyal Tonto. Afterward the grandfather tried to teach them traditional songs, which told the story of the world.

Cross was sent off to the big Indian boarding school in Riverside, California, where he was required to speak English. For lack of practice he forgot his grandfather's songs. Now, as a grandfather himself, he regretted that his granddaughter had to learn the songs from someone else.

After graduating from the boarding school, Cross married, moved to Oakland, California, and went to work in the factories. He drank heavily, almost lost his family, returned to Arizona and the reservation, stopped drinking, and became a Customs tracker and a born-again Christian.

While he talked about his life, the rain ended and the storm rumbled off to the west. The wind was cool and damp; it smelled of wet earth, mesquite, and a trace of skunk. Scattered clouds slid under a half-moon, darkening and brightening the desert. The Baboquivari Mountains rose in a jagged black ridge above us; Cross spoke about I'itoi, the O'odham Creator, who is said to have lived among the peaks. A coyote began to yelp and howl, and the entire valley came alive with a thousand high-pitched answers. The singing lasted for minutes and suddenly died. Cross said, "When I'itoi was making people, he let Coyote help with the cooking. But Coyote didn't pay attention, and he undercooked some and made whites."

Cross must have thought I needed more cooking. He handed me an Atomic Fireball, a peppery candy that burned my mouth. I spit it out and he laughed. He had a bag of Fireballs at his feet. He said they kept him alert during these lonely watches.

Six

Two towns named Nogales stretch along the same narrow valley, about an hour's drive south of Tucson. The one in Arizona is grey and disheveled, but it has grown to about twenty thousand residents and has a new Wal-Mart discount store. Though the people are poor and the schools are uninspired, by some standards the town has prospered. According to Governor Fife Symington, who wrote about Nogales in a *Wall Street Journal* article, taxable retail sales there exceed $300 million a year, which is 50 percent more than in towns of the same size near Phoenix. The taxes impress the governor. What is more, they come from shoppers who do not live in Arizona—Mexicans who stream through the port of entry to buy brand-name goods in U.S. stores. They are allowed through the port because they have steady jobs and thus qualify for short-term border-crossing cards. They prefer brand-name goods for the reasons we all do. They shop in the United States for the cachet and because the prices are lower. Then they go home.

Home is the other Nogales, across the line in Sonora, a city of 100,000 that fills the valley and climbs the slopes on either side. The growth there is vigorous and new. In a reversal of the Arizona pattern, the rich live near the center and the poor occupy the suburban high ground. The poor are called parachutists, as if they had floated down from the sky and dug into the steep hillsides. The reality is less exotic: they come on the bus, seeking employment; they trudge up the hills dragging suitcases and find a spot to live near family or friends. Slowly their camps grow together. The poorest neighborhoods are chaotic, streetless, and so dense that the eye has trouble taking them in. There is no electricity or plumbing. Steep paths wind between the shelters, which are built of scrap plywood, packing crates, car doors, salvaged tin, worn tires, and cardboard. People suffer from malnutrition, disease, parasites. Rainstorms slicken the hillsides and scour the garbage-strewn gulches. Down in the valley the Nogales wash runs with sewage and industrial waste. The mixture flows north into Arizona. Like the New River of Mexicali, it carries sickness and poison. Unlike the New River, it once caught on fire. For all this, some people blame the *maquiladoras*.

Maquiladoras, also called *maquilas,* are a peculiarly Mexican invention—foreign-owned factories that import their materials from the United States, employ Mexican workers (mostly young women) to assemble them, and ship the finished merchandise back north again. The word derives from the Arabic for "measure": after passing through Old World Spanish, where it became the portion received by a miller for grinding grain, it emerged in Mexican usage as the place where the grinding is done. The current scheme was devised in the 1960s as an exception to Mexico's traditional exclusion of foreign companies; it was meant to create employment along the border while protecting Mexican industries from damaging competition. The arrangement boomed after 1982, with the collapse of the peso, when Mexican labor became, as it is today, among the cheapest in the world.

Nearly two thousand *maquilas* now operate in Mexico, most within a few miles of the border. They do not look like much—windowless warehouses in industrial parks— but they employ a half million people and constitute a multibillion-dollar industry that has become Mexico's second largest source of foreign revenue, after oil. Definitions have blurred: as part of liberalization of the economy, Mexico has eased the laws that previously restricted the *maquilas'* access to the Mexican market. For want of more conventional investors, the idea is to use *maquilas* to force competition on a lethargic business community. Free trade and economic growth may eventually eliminate the *maquilas,* but only in the most technical sense. To the extent that Mexico ties its future to the United States, industry will continue to concentrate on the border. The *maquilas* will shed their skins but live on in similar forms. This is an unhappy prospect for people who worry, for instance, about disease and fire in the Nogales wash.

Critics in the United States have used the publicity surrounding the prospect of increased trade to strengthen their attacks on the *maquiladoras.* They accuse the industry of undercutting U.S. labor, exploiting Mexican poverty, and abusing the environment—familiar and legitimate concerns about the irresponsibility of multinational corporations, heightened by proximity. Nogales is Indonesia next door. The presence of seventy *maquilas* there poses a dilemma: we talk about progress, but if Mexico took care of its poor or cleaned up after itself, would our companies still invest there? The *maquila* managers would rather not answer this question. They are business technicians, not advocates, and they are paid to get on with the job.

Frank McGinley is the Nogales plant manager for Coventry Manufacturing, a young Los Angeles–based company that specializes in plastic foam. McGinley lives with his wife and children in a comfortable house in Tucson, and commutes daily to his work in Mexico. At age thirty-eight he is an unassuming, thoughtful man, with a trace of the world-weariness that businessmen develop in poor countries. I met him in central Nogales on a stormy afternoon during a gubernatorial campaign in Sonora. Ubiquitous Institutional Revolutionary Party (PRI) posters proclaimed VAMOS POR MAS PROGRESO! McGinley smiled wryly and said, "Sure, why not?"

"You're not convinced?"

"Tell it to the people living in these shacks—yeah, let's go for more progress."

We navigated the flooded streets to the metal warehouse where he runs his *maquila*. It is a small operation, employing ten men and eight women to produce foam pads for electric car polishers and the cloth bonnets to go with them. McGinley values efficiency: in addition to the weekly output of 6,300 pads and 30,000 bonnets, the plant produces about 1,200 industrial towels from the scraps. The men who work there are energetic teenagers, wiry street kids wearing T-shirts and crucifixes; they form, cut, and glue the pads and stack them on pallets. The women, some of whom are older, make the bonnets with industrial sewing machines arranged in rows under green flourescent lighting. Monday through Friday, work starts at seven and ends at five, with fifteen minutes for coffee in the morning and afternoon, and a half hour for lunch. Coventry gives the workers two weeks' vacation a year, two weeks' pay at Christmas, a production bonus for high volume, and a cash food bonus for being on time. The base wage is about eight dollars a day, which is twice the standard of other *maquilas* in Nogales.

I asked McGinley why he paid such high wages and he answered, to reduce turnover. An unstable work force is one of the greatest problems for U.S. companies in Mexico; at some of the large plants annual turnover approaches 60 percent. Industry blames this self-indulgently on the immaturity of the workers. In truth, their lives are too difficult and they escape if they can. The most courageous move on to the United States. McGinley said that Coventry has a greater sense of responsibility than do other *maquilas*, but he did not claim to have rescued his employees from poverty. He mentioned their large families. When he described the misery of their dirt-floor hovels, I did not ask him to reconcile his dismay with the eight dollars a day. As the United States buys Oscar Sanchez's vegetables, it also buys Coventry's foam pads. The problems facing even his own employees are too large for Frank McGinley to solve—a fact that allows him to avoid feelings of guilt. Hardly pausing for breath, he told me about a seamstress he had hired, a malcontent who tried to organize the workers to strike for still higher wages. McGinley made a few phone calls, found she had caused trouble at other *maquilas,* agonized over it, and confronted her. She quit after the other women warned her that if she continued to agitate, she would not easily find another job. I pointed out to McGinley that under Mexican law, the workers have the right to organize. He answered, but look what we pay already—she was trying to take advantage of us and the others knew it.

We talked about Mexico's environmental regulations, which are nearly as comprehensive as those in the United States and were written with the guidance of the U.S. Environmental Protection Agency. McGinley described the application of the law as "permits for permits' sake." He said, "The enforcement is full of holes. What you do doesn't matter—it's who you know. The guy who arranged the permits for Coventry is friends with the bureaucrats. They worked it out over a cup of coffee."

I said, "Money changing hands?"

He denied it. "We operate by the letter of the law. Most *maquilas* do. Once you start paying *mordida* ('the bite'), it never ends." He pondered this and continued. "Of course, sometimes you might not have a choice. I've heard they come to you and say, 'You need to buy these filters and from this man. If you do, your plant will be in compliance.' "

I brought up the *maquilas'* reputation for environmental recklessness. He said, "There are how many plants now? Sure, some of the shops are dirty, like the chrome-platers who moved to Tecate just so they could dump into the river. But it's too easy to blame the *maquiladoras.* The problem in Mexico is ignorance." He took me to the back room, where the pads are glued together and the molds are washed in acetone. He said, "For instance, we give these guys masks and respirators, but as soon as we turn our backs they take them off. They get mad. They think safety equipment's not macho."

Coventry is the creation of a charismatic salesman named Simon Burrow. When he visits Nogales, he gives short inspirational speeches in English to the assembled employees, and they applaud politely without understanding. In delicate recognition of the similarity between "Burrow" and *"burro,"* they call him Señor Simon. He founded the company in 1981 on the idea of die-cut adhesive-backed shipping pads, which he sold to glass manufacturers to separate their panes. His next idea was even better: a way of cutting foam and putting it on a plastic stick to make a high-tech swab for the computer industry. IBM came through with a huge order and Coventry prospered, manufacturing the swabs in Los Angeles. Three years later disaster struck when a competitor with Korean-made swabs underbid the company and won the IBM contract. Forced to lay off most of its employees, desperate to lower its costs, Coventry moved its production to Mexicali, into an old building next to the boundary fence.

"We didn't know what we were getting into," McGinley explained. "We had contingency plans for bolt cutters in the worst case. We were going to get out right through the fence and take as much of our equipment with us as possible."

"Which 'worst case' do you mean?"

"Expropriation."

That was the old Mexico. Times are better now for American companies. Oddly, the worst case in the new Mexico, should liberalization fail, is civil war. Total collapse is the possibility on everyone's mind.

But the swabs were a perfect match for Mexicali—the manufacturing process was repetitious and labor-intensive. In 1987 Coventry made No. 283 on *Inc.* magazine's list of the fastest-growing private U.S. companies. Mexico was Coventry's salvation. The company found other work that could be done there. "Tedious things like packaging," McGinley said.

And fishing leaders.

"Have you ever wondered what poor soul had to tie those things together? It's us."

In the corporate sense.

Today Coventry employs 120 workers in Mexicali and keeps a few technicians in Los Angeles for the more difficult special jobs. This is the sort of everybody-works arrangement that supporters of global free trade dream of. They say Mexico can be to the United States what Thailand is to Japan—a low-cost production machine in an arrangement that has strengthened the economies of both countries. Critics disagree, believing that it is dangerous to view the Thai-Japanese relationship as a model of unfettered trade. They say Thailand has been crafted by Japan as a platform from which to export to the rest of the world. The crucial difference is this: left to the efficiencies of unregulated trade, Mexico will be used by American companies, mostly to export to the United States. This widens the U.S. trade deficit, destroys American jobs, and further weakens our economy. On the other hand there is civil war. The argument continues.

McGinley argues this: Coventry was forced out of Los Angeles by high wages. If it had moved to Korea or the Philippines, it would have bought its supplies there. Because it moved to Mexico, it buys its supplies in the United States. That may change as Mexico develops and free trade eliminates the duty advantages of buying American. Coventry keeps the Los Angeles operation going because the Mexican workers can't handle the special equipment. That may change, too. In the meantime, the company is still trying to persuade them not to fix production machinery with baling wire.

Coventry's Nogales division is unusual because it ships exclusively to other *maquilas* and not directly to the United States. In other words, those other *maquilas* no longer buy the components from American workers. This is an illustration of the problems that may face the United States if economic liberalization succeeds for Mexico. McGinley answers realistically, that in any case such components could no longer be produced in the United States. He is proud of his creation. He leased the warehouse, got approval from seven Mexican agencies, installed the machines, hired the people, trained them, and got the production going—a one-man show. Then at the Customs broker in Nogales, Arizona, he met a clerk named Maria Lopez. She was thirty, smart, and vigorous. He mentioned that he needed a bilingual secretary. She said, "I'll try to recommend someone. Any other jobs?"

"Yeah, a production manager."

Maria Lopez was born in Nogales, Sonora. Her family moved across the line when she was one, and except for five years in Mexico City, she continued to live in Arizona. She graduated from Nogales High, married, gave birth, divorced, and now was raising a ten-year-old daughter alone. She had owned a children's clothing store, which folded after three years. She had sold real estate until the market collapsed. She still had a little business making pre-tied hair ribbons for girls. Somehow she convinced McGinley that she could run his production line.

Output and quality were low when she went to work at the new plant. She studied the production problems, and with McGinley's encouragement shut down the operation to make the needed improvements. It was an unambiguous way to assume command and apparently it worked—productivity has since almost doubled. Lopez explained this to me while simultaneously teaching one of the men to cut circles from stacks of cloth with an electric blade. The worker wore a chain-mail glove, but even so Lopez fussed. "The minute I turn my back he'll get careless. As if they weren't his fingers."

Speaking of the workers, she said, "At first they wanted to take us for everything we had. They saw we were new at this and they thought maybe we were stupid. But they've learned. They don't abuse, and we don't abuse."

She had not, however, been able to solve the problem of absenteeism. On the Monday of my visit, five of the eighteen workers had not showed up. Lopez said, "In Mexico people are more relaxed. It's hard to understand how easy it is for them just to take the day off. A simple headache is enough. There's not much you can do about it. At first I paid them anyway, but the absenteeism got out of hand. Now they know they will lose the money, and they *need* the money, and still they don't come."

I wondered how the employees had reacted to her. She

said, "There's an idea that Mexican men wouldn't want a woman as a boss, but I'd much rather have men working for me. It was the women who were the most rebellious, who had the most problems relating to me.

"They said, 'You think you can tell us what to do. But everything you know here we've taught you. You can't even sew.'

" 'I'm sorry but I can.'

" 'Then why don't you sit down and sew?'

" 'Because it's not my job.'

"They organized a meeting to throw me out. They went to Frank's office with their complaints: She's nicer to the guys. She'll smile at them and not at us. When she picks out the employee of the week, it's always one of the guys. She's a bitch.

"So I talked to them one by one and finally they started accepting me. It took them about three months, but they've just chilled out completely."

Perhaps not completely, I thought. A young seamstress watched Lopez's back with hard, sullen eyes. She had red lips and fingernails, and wore a coordinated blouse and skirt. Under different circumstances she might have been pretty. She saw me looking and smirked. Later I wondered if I had misread her expressions; she and her mother, who also worked at Coventry, invited me home for coffee at the end of the day. They invited Maria Lopez, too.

Their name is Carbajal. They lived on the side of a hill, in a muddy shantytown turning slowly into a cinder-block slum. They parachuted down twenty years ago. The land was owned by the national railroad and all the neighbors were railroad people. Señor Carbajal was killed on the job when the family was young and his widow now received a small pension that supplemented her earnings from Coventry.

By shantytown standards, they lived comfortably. Five of them—all women—crowded into a two-room shack with cement floors, particleboard walls, and a tin roof. The family had electricity, a console television, a refrigerator, and no plumbing. The place was clean, a refuge from the chaos of the dirt streets.

Maria Lopez and I sat at a small table by the door. Señora Carbajal, whose given name is Francisca, boiled strong black coffee. She was a plump Indian-looking woman in her midforties, who had worked most of her adult life in the big *maquiladoras*. I asked her to describe them.

She said, "There are no breaks. In the lunchrooms there are no microwaves or refrigerators. Instead of giving you a bonus for food, they charge you for your meals."

She could not contain her resentment. Speaking of Foster Grant, where she assembled sunglasses, she said, "I never made more than the minimum wage, but I had to stay because I had five children to support! After I worked there eleven years, my son died and they gave me only three days off!"

She grew calmer as she talked. "I left Foster Grant six years ago. Maybe things have gotten better."

Maria Lopez, who is no apologist for the industry, said, "And afterward, how were the other *maquilas?*"

"They lacked only a whip and chain. You had to work constantly. You couldn't even stand and stretch."

"And Coventry?" I asked, out of duty.

Lopez added earnestly, "You must be completely honest, Francisca."

Señora Carbajal answered, "I expect to be here a long time. I am very happy."

Lopez beamed. She did not seem aware of the gulfs in the room. Earlier, she had said, "In Mexico I am a Mexican," though it was obvious that she was not, that her parents had carried her irrevocably across that line. She spoke warmly to me now, and in English. "Of all the *maquilas* in Nogales, you pick Coventry! Frank McGinley eats his meals with the rest of us. The workers are flattered that he's not intimidated by their poverty. Coventry is a very special place."

I wrote it down. Then I asked Señora Carbajal how she felt living so close for so many years to the riches of the United States. She smiled uncertainly and did not answer. I asked her if she ever visited the other Nogales and she said yes, to shop. I asked for what. She said, "Whatever is on sale. Clothes, beans, rice. Or anything that costs a dollar and contains a lot of laughter."

Grey afternoon light filtered through the window. A porcelain clock painted with cherubs hung on the wall. The television, which was unplugged, was polished like a family shrine. I turned to the once sullen daughter, who sat with softened features on a sofa cuddling her infant girl. She looked away from me shyly. She was nineteen and had already worked four years in the *maquilas*. I asked her if leaving the baby was difficult. She did not answer directly, but said her younger sister helped. Under her mother's gaze, she mumbled that she liked the work.

As Mexico has bound its future to American enterprise, El Paso has bound itself to Ciudad Juárez. Juárez is the cradle of the *maquiladora* industry. At a North American Philips plant the personnel director led me onto the production floor, where 900 young women in white T-shirts sat on stools along semiautomated assembly lines. The personnel director was a middle-aged American, a company man with an unlined face, easily forgotten. He said, "I ask you, does this look like a sweatshop?" The hall was cool, bright, pristine.

I answered, "Impressive." With no standard by which to judge television assembly, what I meant was the presence of so many young women—row upon row of white shirts, red lips, combed black hair, erect backs, quick eyes. They perched their feet on the rungs of the stools in a dazzling display of footwear.

"Twelve thousand sets a day," the man said. "Vertical integration. Sylvania, Magnavox, Philips. Top quality."

The women worked in silence and looked away from us as we walked among them. Their fingers flew nimbly on circuit boards. The machines hissed and clanked. My host explained the details of production.

I interrupted him. "Why women?"

"Concentration and dexterity."

He was affected by them, too. He said proudly, "The white shirts were my idea." He stopped behind one worker and, in a fatherly gesture, laid his hands on her shoulders. "Our plant beauty queen." She was about eighteen and had delicate features thickened by makeup. She turned to smile. We walked on. He said, "Juárez has developed a skilled labor force. The changes in just the last five years are incredible. People who think the Mexicans don't do good work are out of date. Productivity is as high here as anywhere in the world."

Well, almost. Productivity is about 80 percent as high as in the United States. But the labor costs are less than a tenth as much. The "fully loaded" wage of the Philips workers is $1.88 an hour, including taxes, social services, one hot meal a day, and transportation from the slums. This combination of small wages and big results is what upsets the U.S. labor unions. They disagree with the theory that only low-skilled jobs go to Mexico. They say that high skills must inevitably follow.

The Mexicans count on it. By their most optimistic model, the border industrialization will spread south, bringing development and wealth with it. The pioneering enterprises will reshape Mexico around themselves, improving the roads and telephones, training the work force, and raising the standard of living. They will force political changes on the government. They will bootstrap Mexico out of the third world.

In a Juárez hotel I met an American engineer who ridiculed the idea. He was a ferretlike man, badly frustrated. He had been sent by the home office to solve yet another failure on the *maquila* production line. He said, "The corruption kills you. Someone is always demanding a fee. You can say it's unethical, but if you don't pay, after a while you notice that things just aren't happening. These reforms won't amount to much. The comparison to Asia is a pipe dream. Take Korea—you can go there and say,

'Copy this,' and they'll do it, and do it better and cheaper. You don't even have to go there—they come to you! Mexico?" He snorted. "Mexico lacks the midlevel management. Mexico lacks the infrastructure. Most of all, Mexico lacks the entrepreneurial spirit."

I took his doubts across town to Frederico de la Vega, a patrician businessman who was instrumental in bringing the first *maquilas* to Juárez. De la Vega was an affable, thoughtful man in an open-necked shirt. We sat in a genteel restaurant, where many of the patrons knew him. He said, "Nothing is certain. Mexico is built on a system of patronage that will take generations to undo. I myself am worried because the PRI won so overwhelmingly in the last regional elections—we need a strong opposition if for no other reason than to keep the party in line." He smiled reassuringly. "But don't let people convince you that nothing can change in Mexico. Juárez is the perfect example."

I asked him to explain. He said, "Forty years ago, when I came home from college in the United States, I saw my city with fresh eyes. It was nothing but an entertainment center. I don't want to use harsher words."

"The Tijuana syndrome," I said.

"Women, liquor, quick divorces, good times for American soldiers. We fought it for decades and finally won. The irony is that El Paso is still pushing us to develop our tourism. To hell with it. One good factory will provide more jobs than the entire tourist industry. The problem with El Paso is a lack of leadership."

"Go back forty years."

"We thought, this is impossible—how can we raise our families in such a city? We will have to change Juárez or leave it. At first we looked inward and thought of selling to Mexico—brooms, clothing, fertilizer. Eventually we turned to the United States and the *maquiladora* concept. We thought, if we can't develop the city, why not let someone else do it for us?

"It's been a long struggle. At first the *maquiladoras* had a reputation as fly-by-night operations. As little as ten years ago we had to bring over the entire board of the El Paso National Bank to show them what was happening. The *maquiladoras* were spilling over, improving wages, working conditions, and skills for everyone. Today 65 percent of the people in Juárez depend on them, and we have entered the second stage: more high-tech industries, more automation, more joint ventures with Mexicans. The ratio of engineers to workers is increasing. We've gone into the data entry business. The low-tech industries are moving farther south because the real estate has gotten too expensive here. It *is* happening. Of course, change takes time."

Another wealthy Mexican I met in Juárez spoke of the future. He had a wolfish smile. He took the long view and assured me that Mexico is the inevitable partner for American industry. He was in the commercial real estate business. He said, "We have a slump now because of the U.S. recession, but I'm not worried. The *maquilas* are just the beginning. Your labor unionists and environmentalists think they can control the process, but their power is like this." He showed me an inch between thumb and forefinger. "They can play politics. They can squeeze words from us. But we don't *need* formal agreements to have foreign investment. Mexico has only to invite industry and it will come."

"That hasn't proved exactly true," I said.

"Not true? In 1979 there were seventy-five *maquilas* in Juárez, and now there are three hundred. In ten years there will be twice as many. Time will show that Mexico was the great void waiting to be filled."

"If so, it's understandable that American workers are unhappy."

"Yes, of course. History has turned against them."

I admired his frankness. You have only to look at El Paso to see damage caused by economic proximity to Mexico. The city is unkempt and unhappy. Wages are depressed by the availability of cheap Mexican labor. The median family income is 20 percent below the national level, and a third of the residents live in poverty. Unemployment is 11 percent, "which is not bad for a border town," according to a spokesman for the Chamber of Commerce. If not for the army, which has a large base there called Fort Bliss, the numbers would be worse. El Paso is pervaded with a sad boosterism. Television anchors chatter about the city's improved rank on *Money* magazine's livability list of three hundred American places. (El Paso rose to eighty-sixth, which says more about lists than about life on the border.) A business leader said to me, "Take tourism: there's a lot we could do there. We've just got to find a way to get the drivers off the interstate."

The crumbs are for El Paso. The same logic that would take a company there takes it one step farther, across the Rio Grande. This is likely to become even more true as Mexico opens to investment. There are exceptions, of course: industrial space in El Paso is about half as expensive as space in Juárez, so if you are in the warehousing business, you might locate there. But the only reason you would consider it in the first place is its closeness to Mexico. For El Paso, used to thinking of Juárez as that honkytonk next door, the new symbiosis is bitter.

I drove downriver, through the *colonias* that have sprung up outside of El Paso. *Colonia* is Spanish for "colony" or "district." In Mexico it has come to mean the poor and middle-class neighborhoods. In Texas the meaning shifts: the *colonias* are Spanish-speaking suburbs where immigrants buy tiny lots by installment and live in trailers or small substandard houses. El Paso's *colonias* are home to perhaps forty thousand people, 80 percent of whom live in poverty. The settlements sprawl through a flat and treeless world of convulsed dirt. Graffiti marks the walls of crumbled farmhouses. Signs advertising land for sale stick in the earth. The cheapest new districts grow by a fourth every year. Although a regional water district has been formed to serve them, already more than half the households have neither sewage nor safe drinking water. Outhouses and overloaded septic systems taint the wells and threaten the population with epidemic. The residents are aware of the dangers. They wash with dirty water because they must, but buy city water by the gallon for drinking. The water is delivered by vendors who fill barrels at nearby truck stops on the interstate.

I talked to Margarita Flores, a middle-aged woman with close-cropped hair and flowered pants. She and her husband had immigrated from Chihuahua and built a brick and cinder block house in the *colonia* twelve years before, and only now had connected to municipal water and sewage. We sat in her living room, which was ornately decorated. She said, "We finally feel like humans. Before we lived like animals, trying to get water wherever we could. We tried to warn the children, but you know it is very difficult for them to understand. They had rashes and problems with their hair. When they drank the well water, they had stomach problems. It's strange, but we had an easier time in Mexico than Texas."

And proximity to Mexico was partly to blame.

West of El Paso, on U.S. soil, I discovered picketing steelworkers who had walked off the job at a small plant that manufactures sucker rods for oil wells. They had set up a makeshift camp across from the main gate. Seven strikers sat with me in the shade of a tarpaulin. They had a small tent, a basketball hoop, and a portable toilet. They were picketing around the clock on the same shifts they had worked inside. I asked if they would win. One answered with a defiant V-sign and said they had already shut down the plant. Another seemed less sure. He said, "Every morning the manager drives by, and he just looks at us and laughs." He swore. They were burly men in sloppy clothes, and they had been drinking.

The man who did most of the talking had a drooping mustache and an intense, impatient face. He introduced himself simply as Jorge. He said, "All we're asking for is a seventy-five-cent raise, cheap bastards. I make six dollars an hour. My wife works, too, but we run out of money three days before payday."

"No savings," I said.

"I forgot—there's a retirement plan. They give you a hundred dollars a year, a U.S. savings bond."

Someone said drunkenly, "That's the goddamned American way."

Jorge watched me carefully, as if I might have taken offense. He continued, "Same company in Houston, right? Guys doing our job are making ten, twelve dollars an hour."

"For how much longer, do you think?"

He looked somber.

I said, "Of course you realize in Juárez people work for six dollars a day. Your seventy-five-cent raise is what they make in an hour."

"That's what management tells us. I mean they *threaten* us with it. But El Paso is part of the United States, and we want to be part of it, too. We want to live like American citizens."

Seven

Mornings at the Thunderbird restaurant in Marfa, Texas, the tables in the front room are pushed together into a long row. Ranchers in jeans and Stetsons stop by before dawn for coffee. Speaking in half sentences and silences, they talk quietly about rainfall, football, and trouble down on the Rio Grande. Recently they talked again about 2,400 pounds of cocaine found in a red horse trailer at the rodeo grounds and about Rick Thompson, the sheriff implicated in the deal and sentenced to life in prison. He crossed the load at Candelaria, by Nellie Howard's store, and brought it up the steep Pinto Canyon road, two hours to Marfa. Thompson was a tall, handsome man with a big pistol and a white hat. For nineteen years he served as Presidio County sheriff, a symbol of Anglo domination, bringing order to the border. He was a friend to these ranchers. If they feel betrayed by him now, they also sense that his time had come. Their time has come as well. Like so much at the Thunderbird, this is understood without being said. The ranchers are old-fashioned men and they have become bitter, a little sad. They were caught when the economy collapsed, exposing the fictions in their lives. No amount of rain and no foreseeable rise in cattle prices will bring back what they have lost. They blame the Hispanics, who after a hundred years of subjugation have seized political control. They do not think clearly about this but simply assume that the perpetual underclass has now brought ruin on them all. In fact, quite the opposite happened: economic ruin came first, awarding the Hispanics their long-awaited chance to revolt.

I write "Hispanics" only to appear polite. We can be more specific: the new leaders of Marfa are Mexicans. Like Roberto Martínez in San Diego, they have swarthy faces with Indian features and they speak a Spanish not easily understood in Spain. Even the generations long removed from Mexico keep close ties with the south. They themselves do not naturally say Hispanic or use the urban term Chicano. They call themselves Mexican, and because their community is small, they know full well who comes from which side of the border.

This is remote country, West Texas, two hundred miles downriver from El Paso, deep in the shadow of Mexico. Marfa is the seat of Presidio County. It has a stone courthouse, a brick jail, and a single flashing stoplight. Ten years ago, when I lived on the ranch outside of town, the ranchers were at the height of their power. Some mornings I drove in early, and sat with them at the Thunderbird. They had a way of speaking about the Mexicans in the room—the waitresses, cooks, and other customers—as if they weren't present. What they said was sometimes critical, but more usually fond. "Manny, he's a good boy, but look out if he gets mad!" They did not say "boy" in the degrading way of colonial Africa or the American South; they had a kinder use for the word, softened by their habit of calling themselves, grown men, "old boys." But the paternalism was clear. The Mexicans at the Thunderbird participated by pretending not to hear.

Sometimes the ranchers addressed them directly. "Say, Manny, you're quick with the knife, are you?"

"Yessir, I guess, Mr. Larsen."

The Mexicans answered politely since, one way or another, they all worked for the ranchers. Marfa was the smallest kind of town. In 1977 *Texas Monthly* published a story entitled "The Last Frontier—What Texas Once Was, Marfa Still Is." The title stuck in my mind. It meant to praise the Protestant ethic, but it said more about relations between the races. When I moved to Marfa the Mexicans had been in the majority for decades. The ranchers reigned over them. Sheriff Thompson rode herd. Beneath its ordered surface, the town seethed.

Formal decisions were never made at the Thunderbird, and the consensus was rarely spoken. But the power was real. The ranches were big business, and the ranchers wielded budgets of millions of dollars. Sometimes tourists wandered into the restaurant and sat at the small tables along the walls. Misunderstanding the battered pickups and rough clothes, they saw the cowboys at the long table as the simplest Texas rednecks. They did not quite stare. The ranchers loosened their drawls for them; they were confident in those years, and smiled easily. From the Thunderbird their domain spread through the county and beyond.

That's a lot of land. Presidio County borders the Rio Grande for 140 miles, climbs out of Chihuahuan desert over Chinati Mountain and the Sierra Vieja, extends across the mile-high prairie of the Marfa basin, and ends against volcanos that stud the horizons. The neighboring counties are equally large and empty. The ranches are measured not by the acre, but by the square mile, the "section." The biggest have five hundred sections, the smallest perhaps ten. A few have stronghouses built during the Mexican Revolution, when bandits raided across the Rio Grande. The ranchers no longer fortify, but attacks still occur, and people on the ranches must think about security. Most carry guns. They cannot call 911. They are isolated by the scale of the land.

It is the most lovely kind of country. Up on the Marfa basin, the air is dry and the nights are cool. Deer and pronghorn antelope mix with cattle in vast pastures. There are wild sheep, mountain lions, bobcats, and coyotes. The tallest peaks, which rise over eight thousand feet, turn white with snow. When Warner Brothers came in 1955 to film the classic movie *Giant*, the cameramen were careful not to let the mountains show. They created a mythical Texas where the real one would have been better, and invented oil in a landscape saved by the lack of it.

Officially, 6,637 people live in Presidio County. According to the census, which is disputed for undercounting the rush from Mexico, 80 percent of the residents are Hispanic. Four hundred inhabit the ranches and the villages like Candelaria strung along the Rio Grande; the others live in Marfa and in the river town called Presidio, which recently has become the larger of the two. Presidio lies deep in the Rio Grande rift, below the confluence of the Rio Conchos, at an elevation of 2,500 feet. It has dirt streets, empty lots, a few stores, and an international bridge to Ojinaga, Chihuahua. It claims to be the hottest town in the United States. Over the last five years its population has swelled from 1,900 to more than 3,800. The newcomers are Mexicans granted permanent residency under the immigration amnesty program. Most are not yet U.S. citizens and cannot vote. Still, their political weight is felt; by their numbers alone, they speak of the future and promise permanence to Latino power.

Marfa, which lies fifty miles north of the river and a half mile higher, is a wealthier town. From the air it looks like an island of trees in a sea of golden grass. It has adobe and wood-frame houses, shaded streets, Protestant churches, and the highest golf course in Texas. The tracks of the Southern Pacific Railroad divide it east to west. From an airplane you can see trains rolling through that are longer than the town is wide. The trains don't stop here anymore, nor do many tourists. That didn't matter ten years ago when the ranchers had money. The town was comfortable and the population had climbed to over 3,000. Rental houses were hard to find. It is different now: the overbright Chamber of Commerce billboard on the highway attests to Marfa's despair. Storefronts are boarded, houses are abandoned, and nearly a thousand people have left. Of the 2,400 who remain, only a third are Anglos, remnants of the ranching class too old or too entrenched to get out.

The town's largest employer is the Border Patrol, with a "sector headquarters" staff and 150 guards in the field. Mexicans call it a progressive force because it gives them jobs and, for Marfa, pays them well. Another big employer is a company called Loral, which flies one of the Customs radar balloons from a ranch fifteen miles outside of town. Twenty-seven people work at the site. Most of the political figures in town take credit for winning the balloon. At the inaugural ceremony, attended by dignitaries from afar, Mayor Geneveve Prieto Basham mortified the Anglo community with an inarticulate speech. She lost her notes and had to be coached from the side. Mayor Basham is a Mexican-American hairdresser. When I went to see her at city hall, she said, "Of course we don't have that many jobs, but if we did have them, they could be here." I felt sympathy for her. She has been used by her friends to remind the former masters of their fall.

The ground was claimed first by Mexico, then by the Republic of Texas, then by the United States, but it always belonged to the Indians. This is not principle but fact. Above the Rio Grande, roving bands of Apaches and Comanches kept the Spaniards at bay for centuries. Forty-four years after Columbus, in 1536, the shipwrecked Cabeza de Vaca and three companions walked through, southbound after eight years in the New World wilderness. They planted a cross at the junction of the Rio Grande and Conchos, and kept walking. Spaniards returned to the junction in the 1600s and built fortified missions—the presidios of Presidio County—among the peaceful river Indians who farmed the floodplain. Exploratory expeditions penetrated to the north, and despite the splendor of the land, retreated from the onslaughts of hostile tribes. As a result, Marfa's basins and mountains remained uncolonized.

Little is known about the original river Indians. Named

the Patarabueye and Jumano by the Spaniards, they were absorbed by the Mexican culture and by the 1700s had disappeared as a distinguishable society. The fiercer upland peoples held out until the United States assumed title. Soon after the 1848 war with Mexico, Anglo traders and scalp hunters built a private fort on the Rio Grande from which to hunt the Apache. Then in 1854, the U.S. Army established Fort Davis, a cavalry post on Limpia Creek, twenty-three miles north of present-day Marfa. A few settlers arrived, built stronghouses, and began to graze cattle on the open range. One man named Milton Faver ran a herd of ten thousand head. He married a Mexican and employed cowboys from the Rio Grande. It is said he lost his English.

Fort Davis was abandoned during the Civil War. The Indians burned it and drove off the cattlemen. After the war, the soldiers returned and, with the aid of the Texas Rangers, launched a genocidal campaign. By the 1880s, the last Indians had been shipped off to reservations and the land was safe for ranching. In California or New York, where so much has changed, the 1880s seem long ago; but here, where history is sparser, the past lies close in people's minds. I knew a woman who was born at the cavalry post. Fort Davis today is known as "a clean, white town." And there are people in Marfa who still talk with hatred about the Indians, as if they might come back.

The railroad arrived in 1883, and with it came cattlemen fleeing drought in central Texas. Over the next decade, they bought vast tracts of land, fenced them, and built herds. Following the established pattern, they imported Mexicans to do the physical work. The land was lusher then than it is today, and springs flowed where now water is pumped from deep wells. The big families—with names like Means, Mitchell, Espy, and Jones—lived on ranches isolated by hard travel, but they joined together once a year at religious encampments and intermarried so deeply that by today only the most immersed genealogists can trace the connections between the cousins. The genealogists are aging women with collections of journals and old photographs. They know all the family stories and can talk for hours. It is a little sad. Their children have moved away.

Marfa was originally a watering stop for steam locomotives. It was named by a railroad engineer's wife, after the woman servant in Dostoyevski's *The Brothers Karamazov,* which she was reading when she passed through. She looked up from the book, saw a water tank and a few railroad buildings, and she said, "Marfa," and spelled it out. Marfa grew fast and became the county seat. In 1916, during the Mexican Revolution, the army established a base there from which to patrol the border; Candelaria was one of its river outposts. The ranchers prospered. During the Second World War, the army built concrete runways from which bomber crews were taught to fly. The influx of soldiers during the war masked a fundamental change in the county: among the civilians, Mexicans had become the majority. The army left soon after the war. Another forty years passed before the Mexicans finally asserted themselves.

The 1950s marked the beginning of the end for most of the original ranching families. A five-year drought decimated the grasslands. At the same time, the ranchers began moving into town and commuting back out to the ranches to work, a luxury made possible by improved roads, good tires, and powerful pickup trucks. The women were impatient with isolation, and they wanted the social life and the schools of Marfa; the men, too, enjoyed their early-morning coffee together at the Thunderbird. But the ranchers were now distanced from the land and they neglected the fine points of maintenance. Under financial pressure, they began to overgraze. The effect was increasing erosion, the encroachment of the Chihuahuan desert from the south, and an invasion of stubborn bushes like mesquite.

The most serious maladies afflicting the ranches were financial: the growth of families, death and division, the rising value of the land, inheritance taxes, government regulation, interest rates, the downturns of the cattle market, bad business decisions. One by one, the ranchers sold out to oil-rich families from elsewhere. Eager to live the Texas legend, to wear a big hat, the newcomers paid more for the ranches than the ranches could return. But oil money was cheap money, and it saved the aristocracy from debt. If the land prices were inflated, and ultimately destructive, no one complained. The transformation was merciful. The new owners adopted the look and manners of the old, and employed their children as ranch managers. They leased neighboring properties, which allowed the original families to retain parcels for old time's sake. And some of the biggest ranches never had to sell; oil money married into them, propping them up from the inside. By the early 1980s, after decades of living a fiction, Marfa had become a caricature.

For three days in 1983, the town celebrated its centennial. A singing airline pilot named Claudia Jones recorded an album entitled *Where the Heck Is Marfa, Texas?* But everyone who counted already knew: people flew in for the celebration from the farthest corners of the United States. There were western dances, Mexican dances, barbecues, rodeos, parades, and helicopter rides. The ranchers wore centennial belt buckles and their best hats, and rode prancing horses in the streets. Marfa the myth shone gloriously.

The illusions ended in 1985 after oil prices tumbled. Stuck with ranches they could neither afford to keep nor afford to sell, the oilmen stopped spending. Marfa's economy died and people began leaving. The masters had done themselves in. With the opportunity thrust on them, the Mexicans finally rose up. Within two years of the oil collapse Geneveve Prieto Basham had won the mayoral election. The evening of her victory, Mexican citizens cruised the streets blowing their horns. They were jubilant and angry, and after a hundred years they let it show. Some made their way to the Catholic church and rang the bells. I've heard many versions of that night. The bells could be heard throughout town. They rang for an hour, while the ranchers sat like prisoners in their houses.

I returned to Marfa to learn about the changes. At a trailer park on the south edge of town, I met Phil Cordero, one of the new county commissioners. Cordero was loud and bombastic, a plumber by trade. His first words to me were, "The only perfect man in the world was crucified. Now we're pissing and shitting on the substance of life—water."

The county judge, who had taken me to meet him,

interpreted: "We're not perfect. We need to improve the system."

I asked Cordero if he had plans to develop Marfa.

He said, "Take this weather now. If we could bottle it, we'd all be millionaires."

The judge said: "Honestly, no."

But Cordero was no idiot. His loudness was a strength, his bravura a form of self-preservation. When I asked him about relations between the races, he said, "The ranchers figured they'd bring the Mexicans up here and benefit from us. They were strong and we were weak. If you detect weakness in someone, you'll use it, you'll dominate him. But it's different now. The ranchers sort of faded away. And we learned that education brings deliverance."

I wanted him to describe the old relationship, the one I had known from the Anglo side. I said, "I remember. It was paternalistic, not brutal."

"As long as we kept saying, 'Thank you, señor.' "

"You had to be grateful."

"And loyal."

I said, "Through generations."

He nodded. "The rancher would say, 'Hey, Pedro, school's gonna start pretty soon, here's some clothes for the kids, some tires for the car.' It was this charity thing, and it made a lot of our old people feel secure. If the kids got sick, Mr. Jones would provide and they'd be indebted forever.

"But we figured it out. At parties they tried this, 'Hey, Pedro, here's some money, go get some more beer,' and we started saying, 'No way.' Then suddenly we went from being good boys to being troublemakers."

"It must have been hard for you in such a small town."

He denied it. "When I first got elected, they tried black-balling me, but since I'm the only plumber doing service calls I survived. One day there was a group talking about me at the Thunderbird. So I walked across the street to Pierce Motors, and I bought a new pickup right in front of their eyes. They could see they weren't hurting me too much."

But they hurt others. I talked to a shopkeeper who spoke of the years when Anglos controlled the city government. He said, "They never bought here. They always went out of town and bought from someone else. They didn't sit around saying, 'Let's make sure we don't give it to a Mexican.' It was just their way of doing business. They didn't think a Mexican could do a good job or have anything worth buying."

"You hold it against them?"

He smiled angrily. "Not just me."

The oldest and poorest barrio in Marfa lies on the east side, across the dry creek from the main body of town. It is a dispersed neighborhood of adobe houses and junked cars. Until recently it had few paved streets and little sewage or municipal water. Anglos call it Mexico Town, or Little Chihuahua. Mexicans call it Sal Si Puedes, which means "Get Out If You Can." In a backyard there, I met furtively with a grey-haired man, who wanted assurances that I would not use his name. He seemed unsure of his new freedom. He said, "With the economy so damned bad now, you can't afford to speak out. You think, 'Those sons-a-bitches,' but you try to hold it in."

"You mean about the Anglos?" I asked.

"If they find out I'm talking to you, they'll blackball me."

It was the second time I had heard that term. I said, "But you already have a reputation as a militant."

He snorted. "Why, because neighbors met at my house? Because I don't jump when a gringo says jump?"

I asked about the past. He said, "In the forties there was a town pool we couldn't swim in except when they were changing the water. There was a restaurant called the Longhorn with a sign that said NO DOGS OR MEXICANS ALLOWED."

I said, "In fairness to Marfa, the same sign was posted all over Texas."

He answered, "Once you're treated that way, you never forget."

He was filled with hatred. Talking only made it worse.

I asked him about the political changes. He said, "It used to be nobody would see any Mexicans working at the courthouse. Now the sons-a-bitches, if they want something they have to go through us."

I wondered about his school days. He said, "Blackwell," meaning the segregated elementary school that closed in 1964. The high school was never segregated because few Mexican children made it that far. He said, "You should have been here last month for the Blackwell reunion. People came from out of town. They could have told you why they left."

"Why did they?"

"It was the only way to get ahead. The sheriff harassed you. The bank wouldn't give you a loan because your daddy didn't make enough. Some white guy had to cosign for you—like fifty bucks for an old car."

"And why didn't *you* leave?"

He shook his head. "Stupid, I guess."

It is probably no coincidence that one person who did leave, and who came back after twenty years, seemed to feel little of this frustration. His name was Mario Acosta, age forty-two, in a white shirt and tie. I met him at Marfa Elementary, of which he was then the principal.

Marfa Elementary is a bilingual school in the heart of the Anglo district; of its 347 students (kindergarten through eighth grade), 85 percent are Hispanic. Acosta lived nearby, with his Anglo wife and young daughter. To a Marfan from the 1950s it all would have seemed strange.

Acosta did not dwell on racial division. He translated Sal Si Puedes for me, "Get Out If You Can," and derived the name from the fact that before the bridge was built, when the creek flooded, there was no way out of the neighborhood. I was struck by the simplicity of his reasoning. It seemed to spring across a thirty-year gap, from the innocence of a childhood in more cautious times.

Sal Si Puedes is where he grew up with his parents and four sisters. His father, born in Marfa, worked as an assistant mechanic for the General Motors dealer, now closed. His mother took in laundry. Neither parent had more than a first-grade education, and neither spoke English. The family lived in a three-room adobe house with no indoor plumbing. Acosta said to me, "I didn't think I was living in hardship. There was always someone home, I always had my family. The first time I was even aware of poverty was when my father gave a used battery to a friend so he could sell it to the junk dealer to buy beans."

They had chickens in the yard and a gas stove in the kitchen. Weekends, they drove the 1939 Ford to Odessa to see relatives. They drove to fiestas across the river in Ojinaga. Once they visited San Antonio. When Mario was six, he started first grade at Blackwell. The teachers were Anglo women; he now believes they were dedicated and competent.

I asked him how segregation worked. He said, "The dividing line was the railroad. Because we lived on the north side, we had the right to attend Marfa Elementary, but we chose to go to Blackwell. It was what we knew."

Like all the children at Blackwell, he was kept in first grade for two years to learn English. The students were not allowed to speak Spanish. Mario was caught only once, at a flag ceremony in the courtyard. The principal whacked the boy he was talking to on the head with his ring finger. It does not seem too unfair.

Blackwell closed when Mario was in eighth grade. One morning all two hundred Blackwell students walked in a procession across town to Marfa Elementary. They carried their books. At Marfa Elementary they were segregated by classroom but allowed to mix with the Anglos in the cafeteria and on the playing field. For Mario, segregation ended the next year in high school.

I asked, "How did it feel to be with the ranchers' kids, knowing their attitudes?"

He was unhappy with the question. "Sure, there were animosities. I was aware of the divisions. But my father taught me I could compete with anyone."

His father insisted that Mario concentrate on his studies, and despite the family's poverty, he refused to let him take even a part-time job. Mario graduated in 1969 in a class of fifty-six seniors, of whom half were Mexican; he still spoke more Spanish than English. He planned to enlist in the marines. But his father borrowed money and said, "You're going to Sul Ross." Sul Ross is the state university in neighboring Alpine, named after a Texas governor. Mario graduated from it, became a teacher and a coach, moved to central Texas, got a master's degree, and worked his way into school administration.

He returned to Marfa in 1990 because he felt he could help. There were twenty-one applicants for the principal's position. He knew about the changes in town. "I told the board I wanted the job, but not because I was Hispanic."

I said, "The board itself is Hispanic." Then I worried how it had sounded.

He seemed equally uneasy. "I've always known I'm an American, a Texan, and from Marfa, Texas."

"I realize you're in a delicate position."

"The problem is when it gets political."

I thought, and how can it not?

We went to Sal Si Puedes to meet his parents, who still lived in the adobe house of his childhood. The tiny front room was dim but neat. An air conditioner kept it cool despite the seven-foot ceiling. I studied framed photographs of the children. We sat stiffly. At age seventy, the father was tall, gaunt, and unshaven. He waited for me to ask him a question. I said, "I want to know about the old days."

He answered in Spanish. "The reason I didn't go to school was I didn't have any clothes to go to school. For most people this was true." Then apparently he thought better of talking to me. Staring at the floor, he lapsed into gloomy silence.

His wife, two years younger, with grey, frizzy hair, was less cautious. She said, "We paid $700 for this house in 1955. I ironed to help out. When Mario was in high school, I cleaned the firehouse one day a week for $200 a year. It was never easy in Marfa. I knew the ranchers didn't like progress. They wanted to keep things like they were. The Coca-Cola plant moved to Alpine. We lost the clothing factory. Marfa even had the chance to get a hospital and the college, but the ranchers voted it down."

The ranchers tell a different history with equal conviction, but I was not surprised by her bitterness. She said, "I wanted my children to know that here, there was no opportunity."

Acosta tried to explain away his mother's outburst. "It used to be if you did not have land, you were nothing. But that has changed."

I said to the old woman, "Finally you have the power."

She nodded but did not seem to care. I thought she was still too angry to be pleased by her son's rise to local prominence. When recently he resigned and moved to another school district, I think she hoped he had made good his escape.

A century of unhappiness has risen to the surface. I met the impoverished heiress of a ranching family that had lost its land. She had spent some years in San Francisco, and had adopted the language and demeanor of a city woman. I asked her why she had returned to live in Marfa. She sighed. "I don't know. I think maybe we all idealize the towns of our youth." But she no longer did.

Speaking of the neighboring county seats, she said, "Alpine is transient. Fort Davis is cliquish. And Marfa? Marfa is just plain hateful."

Her vehemence felt too intimate. I said something distancing about Mario Acosta and integration in the schools. She answered, "When I was in school, the Mexican and Anglo kids were friendly then too. The problem is what happens afterward. Most of the people I grew up with are consumed with their hatreds. I really have no hope for the future."

Nor does Donald Judd, the world-famous sculptor who moved to Marfa from New York twenty years ago, and who lives at the center of town. To me he said, "The Anglos are degenerate colonials, like the characters in British novels. They've developed an end-of-the-world attitude. They want to take the whole place down with them."

I remembered an exchange in which a ranching woman had found confirmation in the words of an old and loyal Mexican maid. The maid was disgusted with the new Hispanic leadership. She said, "They're gonna screw it up so bad, they're gonna *have* to give it back to the ranchers." The ranching woman was encouraged by this prediction, especially because it was spoken by a Mexican, and she now looked forward to the fiscal collapse of the city. Colonial history, of course, teaches a different lesson: no matter what their failings, liberated nations have shown no desire to return to their European masters.

I mentioned this to Judd and he nodded quietly. Judd has a grey beard, liquid eyes, and a shy, intellectual manner. He designs austere sculptures of metal, wood, and concrete. He moved to Marfa to escape the commercialization of New York and to find a place for the permanent installation of his work. Like most outsiders to Marfa, he sympathized with the Mexicans. Although he had made a fortune with his art, he rented a small house in Sal Si Puedes. I am sure he paid generously for it. Later he hired locals, most Mexican, to install his art, and offered them medical benefits and big salaries. He created a nonprofit foundation for the installation of more works, directed it to buy the old army base and much of the abandoned downtown, and made a point of keeping the properties on the tax rolls. He tried to bring new ideas to the town. He sent his children to the public schools. He was too wise to expect gratitude but perhaps too absorbed to anticipate the hostility he engendered. He ran for the school board and was crushed. The ranchers said he was subversive. The Mexicans called him a fool.

The compound that is his main residence takes up a full city block. For reasons of art and architecture, he surrounded it with nine-foot adobe walls. But Marfans don't care about his aesthetics; they see only the outside of the walls, and they feel excluded and insulted. It is true that Judd has made himself unapproachable, and that, even for him, his walls have come to symbolize a withdrawal from the town. I asked him about the Mexican revolt and he shrugged. "It was necessary. But you can see what happens. We don't have a real community here. We did have one and it wasn't nice. Maybe now we'll have nothing."

While visiting his home in Europe, Judd wrote this about Marfa, published in a collection of his essays on architecture:

Although most of the houses in the town are made of adobe the technique had been forgotten. I hired legal workers from Mexico to make adobes and to lay them. The reason for the neglect of the technique is that everyone, Anglo-Americans always and Mexican-Americans now, consider the material unstylish. To the Anglo-Americans it is poor and Mexican; to the Mexican-Americans it is poor and un-American; to both it is not upwardly-mobile, not middle-class. There is more status in aluminum siding and plastic walnut paneling. In this case the preference is not due to availability and lower cost—the siding and paneling are more expensive. "Store-bought" things represent the greater society, the society that somewhere is supposed to know more than the consumers, who nevertheless think they are making a decision . . . when they choose between flowers and diamonds on the plastic tablecloth. My farming neighbors here in Europe have plastic dwarfs in front of their houses. In Texas they use plastic ducks. The claim these represent is large and vague; the identification to outsiders is small and precise. This is a big subject. It certainly pertains to equally vague politics. All over the world there are plastic dwarfs and ducks. There is supposed to be two and a half times as many dwarfs as Austrians in Austria. It's possible that there are 30 million ducks in Texas. Anyway Texas is paved with plastic walnut paneling, whose connotation isn't precise: all classes love it.

Judd is fated to such bitterness. I understood it better after taking a ride through the desert in one of the foundation trucks with two of his Mexican employees. They were at once rebellious and servile. They drank beer and threw the empty cans out the windows until they came to Judd's property, where they threw the cans on the floor. "He wants to protect nature or something," one said, and laughed. The truck was a big Dodge. They drove it hard, banging it through the creeks. The other said, "I hate this truck." I asked why. Delighted, he answered, "I hate this truck because it belongs to the boss." I concluded that he hated Judd as well.

Judd knows. He called the Mexicans hopelessly uneducated, which is true. Then he said, "They despise the land. They don't want to stay down on the river. It's not the thing to do. They want to be up here in Marfa and watch TV. It's no different than New York, where you don't want to stay on Mulberry Street and tend the store, where you want to escape to Yonkers and some definition of affluence."

Judd works the process in reverse. Having fled New York for Marfa, he now flees farther, down to the Rio Grande and the seventy square miles of desert and mountain he calls his ranch. He has fenced the property's periphery, not to keep livestock in, but to keep people out. Nearby, he recently purchased the five sections of riverland that include the store and the entire village of Candelaria. Nellie Howard and her sister, Marian, sold it to him. If he does not plan to tend the store himself, he wants to make it better and cheaper, and sell fresh food there.

Candelaria is Judd's answer to Marfa. The villagers still live close to the land, build their houses of adobe, and paint the interior walls a simple white. The store's single room is tall, dim, and cool. Sunlight filters through a screen door and a row of dusty windows high on the west wall. It is a big room with a worn wooden floor. You could hold a dance in there, though I don't imagine the old sisters would approve. I never heard music in their store, only the chirping of birds in the cottonwood outside. But Judd is a new generation and he throws a good party. He told me the villagers had nothing to worry about from him, though he might pay them to remove their junked cars. He talked about organizing a farming cooperative, and maybe bottling the well water.

The old sisters will retire to Marfa. When I spoke to them about the sale of Candelaria, they expressed satisfaction with Judd's plan to keep the store open, but chuckled about his idea of enlisting the Mexicans in a cooperative. Nellie Howard said, "We finally taught them not to lean on the counters or spit on the floors." Marian said, "Oh, they'll work him over!" She thought this would do Judd a world of good. I believed her, but then I think in the long term the same is true for Marfa and for the United States as well.

It is difficult to fix the start of the revolt and too early to declare its end. At the silver mine in Shafter, between Marfa and Presidio, Mexican laborers rioted in 1893 and were suppressed by the Texas Rangers. Twenty years later, during the revolution, Mexican ranch hands sheltered bandits who raided from across the river. It was an unforgivable betrayal. During the wave of anti-Mexican sentiment that swept Texas, Marfa imposed a curfew on its Mexicans from dusk to dawn.

The most notorious raid occurred at the end of 1917, the year Pancho Villa made a mockery of Pershing's Chihuahua expedition. On Christmas Day, bandits hit the Brite Ranch, about thirty miles southeast of Marfa. The ranch, which is still one of the largest holdings in the area, was a fiefdom with its own store and post office. The Brites had gone to Marfa for Christmas, leaving their foreman and his family at the headquarters. At dawn fifty Mexicans rode in shooting, yelling "Death to the Gringos!" The foreman's father shot back, killing an attacker. The family blockaded itself in the house, which was fortified, and the bandits, who had no intention of harming the Brites' Mexican workers, spent a few hours looting the store and rounding up the ranch's prize horses.

Midmorning, a Marfa minister drove up in a car with his wife and two other women. They were seized but later released when the bandits learned their captive was a man of God. The minister and women scurried into the foreman's house, where the minister said a quick prayer and picked up a gun. Soon afterward another Christmas guest approached in a car, spotted the raiders, and sped off to raise the alarm. At about the same time, a neighbor who had heard the gunshots from several miles away telephoned the army in Marfa.

The next visitor was an Irish mule-driver named Mickey Welch, who arrived with the mail wagon and was immediately fired upon. After both his passengers were killed, Welch surrendered. The Mexicans forced him to unhitch his mules. When he cursed them, they dragged him into the back of the store, hung him from the rafters, and cut his throat.

A Marfa posse arrived by car around noon, but the bandits escaped on horseback down steep canyon walls where no car could follow, to the Rio Grande. The next day the U.S. Cavalry caught up with them in Mexico and killed ten. But ten was not enough.

For days afterward, armed men patrolled the Marfa streets, while women and children hid in the safety of the courthouse. Two hundred ranchers and rangers met at the Stockman's Club and formed a vigilance committee to register and disarm all the Mexicans in five counties. According to Glen Justice, a historian at Midland College who has written about the killings, one of the Brite defenders said, "We used to contend with the Comanches every light moon. We knew what we were going up against when we seen a bunch of Comanches; there were two things to do, fight or run. You meet a bunch of Mexicans and you don't know what you are going up against; whether they are civilized or not." Similar fears pervade the border today. The timid response has always been to assume the worst.

One month after the Brite raid, on the night of January 27, 1918, Marfa had its vengeance. A group of fifty rangers and deputized ranchers, accompanied by another forty U.S. Cavalrymen, surrounded a squalid village called Porvenir, which lay in Presidio County on the north bank of the Rio Grande. Porvenir was home to 140 Mexican farmers, many of whom were U.S. citizens. It had a school but no post office. The nearest store was a day's ride away, at the Brite ranch. The lawmen called Porvenir a squatters' camp and bandits' den. They had raided it several nights before, and had found two rifles and a shotgun, and three men wearing shoes of the type stolen from the Brite store. For the lawmen, this was proof enough. The soldiers, who came from a nearby post, knew the residents by name, and vouched for their innocence. Nonetheless, they had orders from headquarters in Marfa to assist the posse.

The night was cold. Justice writes that the rangers were drinking whiskey. They stood aside while the soldiers rounded up the villagers and searched their huts. The search turned up nothing of interest. Afterward, the rangers asked to be left with the Mexicans for additional questioning. The soldiers protested but withdrew. No sooner had they disappeared than the rangers separated the men from the women and children. The villagers begged for their lives. The rangers selected fifteen men, ranging in age from seventeen to seventy-two, marched them into the night, and shot them dead.

Although news of the massacre eventually leaked out, embarrassing both the rangers and the cavalry, no criminal charges were brought. Ranchers agreed that the killing was a job well done and that the "river Mexicans" had finally been taught a lesson. Among the Mexicans, the first reaction was a panic that caused hundreds to flee south across the Rio Grande. The longer consequence is the hatred that only now is visible. Anglos are not the only ones in Marfa with long memories. Old women in Sal Si Puedes still mourn the victims. When the ranchers say "Remember the Alamo!" the Mexicans mutter "Remember Porvenir."

Marfa's Mexicans fought in the U.S Army during the Second World War and Korea, and when they came home they talked about another way of living. Vietnam heightened their resentment: all three Marfa boys killed there were Mexican-Americans, while many of the ranchers' sons avoided service altogether.

In November 1969, Crystal City revolted. It was a farming town three hundred miles southeast of Marfa, in the humid Winter Garden area of Texas. In some respects it was similar to Marfa: though Mexicans comprised 85 percent of the population, Anglos owned 95 percent of the surrounding land and controlled the government. Among Mexicans, the median for years of education was 2.3; of those who made it to high school, 70 percent dropped out.

The revolt started in the high school among would-be cheerleaders. The school had a long-standing rule that only those girls whose mothers had been cheerleaders could themselves qualify for the squad. What this meant, of course, was that no Mexicans need try out. There were similar bars to other extracurricular activities. Outraged by the school board's refusal to listen to their grievances, and supported by their parents, 1,700 students went on strike. That was just the start. Within six months the Mexicans had taken control not only of the school board, but also of the city council. And their rebellion spread. One after the other, the neighboring towns succumbed to it.

But West Texas was far away. Eight years after Crystal City, in 1977, the Mexicans of Marfa held their first political meeting. The following year, in 1978, they organized a registration drive to defeat Rick Thompson, the legendary sheriff. Thompson had a reputation of being rough on Mexicans and allowing beatings in the jail. Against him, the Mexicans ran a city cop named Rodriguez. When the ballots were counted, Rodriguez had won by sixteen votes.

Thompson went to court and successfully contested the election by arguing that Rodriguez was not a resident of the county: though he worked in Marfa and stayed with his girlfriend there, his main domicile was in Fort Stockton, a hundred miles away. After losing the election, Rodriguez also lost his regular job and had to leave town. People still talk about the anger in the streets.

I found it odd that Thompson won the successive elections with increasing support from the Mexican community. I thought perhaps this was because he had reformed. But Mexicans in Marfa told me he won because they were afraid, and they no longer dared organize against him. He knew too much about too many of them. Even now they dare speak about him only because he has been safely removed to Federal prison on smuggling convictions. They are, of course, delighted with his downfall. His replacement was appointed by a Hispanic state district judge who was Thompson's political enemy. The new sheriff is a quiet and gentle man named Abe Gonzales, who makes a show of not wearing a gun. This seems foolish to some of the Anglos, who believe such passivity will get him killed. The border is a dangerous place. I have wondered, however, how the Anglos would feel if Sheriff Gonzales were more forceful.

The mutiny has not been easy on anyone. I talked to a Mexican who said, "We have plenty of good people here in Marfa, but we have yet to see the real quality come to the surface. It's like any revolution—the smart ones hang back and don't take risks. It's the fools who rush to the front to lead the changes."

He meant Bobby Martinez, a grocer who was elected

mayor in 1981. Fool is an unfair characterization; Martinez perhaps underestimated the difficulty of change. Marfa's government is a triumvirate of the mayor and two city commissioners, serving unlimited two-year terms. Both commissioners under Martinez were Anglos, and they thwarted him. Reelected in 1983, Martinez found himself in the same political bind. Halfway through his second term, despised by the Anglos and increasingly unpopular among the Mexicans, he resigned in frustration. For a few years afterwards the Anglos rallied.

A special election was called, and the Anglos struck with vengeance. They elected Jane Shurley, a beautiful, rich blonde, the wife of a rancher and daughter of an oilman—the epitome of Marfa's upper class. Shurley served a one-year term, and was reelected in 1985. She ruled in imperial style, through all-Anglo commissions. Some people still insist she was a good mayor: she won state grants, and began to pave the streets of Sal Si Puedes. Nonetheless, she was sharp-tongued and haughty, and she developed a reputation as an unrepentant racist. A rumor went through the Mexican community that she had yelled, "Kill the greasers!" at a football game. The rumor was patently untrue, but it was believed. In response, Mexicans began to yell, "Kill the gringos!" Ghosts of the Brite Ranch hung over the town.

The economy collapsed during Shurley's second term, and the ranchers began to quarrel. By the time of the watershed 1987 election, some Anglos were angry enough to abstain from voting. The Mexicans were even angrier, and were delighted to find in Geneveve Prieto Basham a hairdresser willing to take on a queen. Bumper stickers appeared reading VIVA VEVA! Shurley's defeat was resounding. The bells at the Catholic church tolled. Since Basham was accompanied into office by a commissioner named Alvarado, a Mexican coalition had finally taken city hall.

Meanwhile, ex-mayor Bobby Martinez had been elected judge, the chief executive of Presidio County. Martinez won the election with support from the town of Presidio. But it did not finish well for him. By the end of his four years, the rebellion had consumed him. He is a sad figure now, tentative and grey-haired. When I went to see him, and mentioned the immigrants who once worked on the ranches, he said, "We made them all citizens," as if he regretted it. Presidio grew during his term, as did the confidence of the Mexican-American electorate. Martinez was too cautious, and he became tainted by his association with the remnants of Anglo power. He was accused of selling out, of courting Anglo support. It was probably true. He was accused of having turned into a bigot against his own people. By then he was a defeated man. The loss of the Democratic primary in 1990 only confirmed it. Geneveve Prieto Basham kindly gave him a job as the town administrator. He told me he was grateful.

Perceptions and allegiances have shifted in unexpected ways. Some people hope that a middle ground can be found. Monroe Elms, the man who defeated Martinez in the Democratic primary, and who ultimately won the election for county judge with strong Mexican support, looks and talks like a West Texas cowboy. At age thirty-six, he has red hair and white skin. You would never guess that his grandmother was a Mexican—therefore he tells you. He campaigned in fluent Spanish and allied himself fiercely with the Mexican side. This was more than political strategy; Elms's wife is Mexican and he speaks Spanish at home. He lives in Shafter, by the old silver mine, and because of his distaste for the ranchers, refuses to move to Marfa. Years ago, he was in the first wave that conquered the school board when taxes were low and the schools were in need of repair. He tells about a rancher who said, "Monroe, if you raise the taxes, all you'll do is ruin good sheepherders." Elms knows he is disliked by the ranchers. Speaking of his tenure as the judge, he told me, "Their problem is they don't have a flunky anymore."

The ranchers told me Elms is worse than a Mexican. They call him a "squaw man." The opponent they supported in the 1990 election is Elms's first cousin, Jake Brisbin, a wounded Vietnam veteran who is also one-quarter Mexican. Brisbin heads the local cable television company. He ran as a Republican and a friend of the Shurleys, and received more contributions than he could spend. As a child he had been forbidden to mention his Mexican blood. But during the last fight he, too, campaigned in Spanish and played on his border heritage.

Eight

Ojinaga, Chihuahua, deserves its reputation as one tough border town. Seen from the Marfa highway, it lies past Presidio, Texas, beyond the green trace of the Rio Grande. Smoke from burning tires and cooking fires fades into the cloudless sky. The town covers a hill and spreads beyond into the desert. Dust colors it khaki, like the desert, and makes it look smaller and less important than it is. This camouflage is appropriate: thirty thousand people live in Ojinaga, and thousands more inhabit its dependent villages along 250 miles of the Rio Grande, and directly or indirectly most of these people make their living from the illegal trade in narcotics. Some have become rich. You see their houses in town and by the river—modern mansions with black iron gates and satellite dishes, incongruous in a desolate land. Among the young and the poor, such displays arouse mostly admiration.

Traffickers are the folk heroes of the new Mexico. They spread their abundance about, knowing that generosity is one key to their success. Their largesse has not been healthy for a nation long weakened by opportunism and corruption, where government cannot resist temptation. While presidents and professors plot the course of history, these details make a mockery of political science. Here as in Colombia or Peru, brutality reigns when narcotics take control. That is what happened to Ojinaga. You could stand in Texas and hear the weapons firing across the Rio Grande.

Smuggling is a natural activity in a desert whose only resource is the border itself. The first smugglers trafficked in wax extracted from the candelilla plant, a thick-stemmed bush that grows in the Chihuahuan mountains. Candelilla's scientific name is *Euphorbia antisyphilitica*, because it once was used to treat venereal disease. More practically, its wax is used in the manufacture of chewing gum and household polishes. The wax is tan, dense, and odorless. Though it has never been illegal in either country, in Mexico it was considered to be a national resource and was controlled by a government monopoly that enforced low market prices. Villagers therefore harvested the plant in secret and smuggled the wax out of Mexico. The government answered with a special police force, the hated *forestales,* who wandered the desert looking for smoke from the wax extraction process. There were gunfights and killings, but for people used to hardship, the money to be made in the United States made the risk worthwhile. Their grandchildren today take greater risks for still greater rewards. The candelilla trade continues, much reduced, and now seems merely quaint. Wax harvested in Mexico is sold to storekeepers on the U.S. side, and resold to an old man from Presidio who drives along the river road buying chunks for eighty-two cents a pound. The buyer took me to his garage and showed me five thousand pounds in stacked burlap sacks. He was enthusiastic, and insisted that I keep a sample for myself. He gave me about two dollars' worth, which was more than I wanted.

For precisely that reason, ambitious smugglers were never satisfied with candelilla wax. They herded stolen Mexican cattle across the river, and during the Prohibition of the 1920s they dealt in sotol, the liquor made from a cactus of the same name. During the Second World War, Ojinaga ran hundred-mule caravans of rationed goods north at night through the rugged ranchland. Smuggling was hard work. The years following the war brought a more profitable but still small trade in morphine and heroin. In 1948 only five thousand people lived in Ojinaga.

By the early 1970s Ojinaga was booming. Drugs had taken over, and twenty thousand people had come to town. The traffickers were moving big loads of marijuana, a crop well suited to the climate and politics of Mexico. Because of the family ties between Ojinaga and the immigrant communities of Texas and New Mexico, the distribution networks were efficient and difficult to penetrate. Payment was in cash and weapons. The new "mules" were not four-legged animals, but ordinary-looking people carrying narcotics strapped under their arms, in false compartments in their cars, or simply beneath tarpaulins in the back of their pickups. Some were free-lance distributors who bought small loads on the river and sold to dealers farther north. Others were farmworkers paid directly by the traffickers in Mexico. Then as now, the biggest men were careful to stay behind the border, beyond the grasp of U.S. authorities.

Over the years, the racket in Ojinaga was organized under a succession of captains. The other traffickers did not have to work for them but were required to recognize their supremacy and to pay them a percentage of the business they did in the territory, which extended for hundreds of miles along the Rio Grande. The captaincy therefore brought riches but also responsibilities. Most burdensome were the protection payments to state and federal officials in Chihuahua City, which the captain made on behalf of everyone. Locally, he was expected to replace the government and the traditional patronage that he had corrupted: like the heads of Sicilian crime families, he helped the indigent, decided small disputes, and perhaps improved a village road, or dug a well, or provided for a public fiesta. Finally, he had to enforce discipline within the unruly ranks of the drug business. This was something the captains did naturally and well. Traffickers who rebelled or tried to avoid the percentage were found out, tortured, and executed. Their deaths served as public warnings. Though the identity of the killers was usually known, the crimes went unpunished. Relations with the authorities were uneasy but manageable: the police staged raids, but later released the prisoners; they burned marijuana fields on national television, but only after the harvest. Even the army was involved: it stood guard over the most valuable loads and protected the top men from one another. In 1974 the traffickers won the mayoral election and replaced the entire municipal police force. Afterward the town belonged to them and they swaggered openly through the streets carrying automatic rifles. In 1981 the greatest of them all, Pablo Acosta, took control.

Acosta was born in 1937 near the village of Santa Elena,

about a hundred miles downriver from Ojinaga, across the Rio Grande from Big Bend National Park. His grandfather and father were American citizens, born in Texas. They homesteaded in Mexico during the revolution, and later slipped back and forth across the border, picking crops and smuggling sotol and candelilla wax. Young Acosta attended elementary school in Mexico, and learned to read and write. At the age of twelve, he joined his father on the migrant trails of Texas and eastern New Mexico. It was a tough life. He learned to drink and fight, and he began to have trouble with the law. In 1958, at age twenty-one, he witnessed his father's murder at a bar in Fort Stockton, Texas. He continued to work in the fields and in cotton gins. In 1964, as the son of an American, he was awarded U.S. citizenship. Three months later in Lovington, New Mexico, he shot a man in the chest. He served thirty days in jail.

He became a roofing contractor, married a girl from Ojinaga, and brought her back to live in Odessa, Texas. They scraped by. In 1968, at age thirty-one, he tried to smuggle an ounce of heroin into the country, but was betrayed, and was arrested on the highway near Marfa. He spent five years in federal penitentiaries, where he made more reliable friends. Upon his release in 1973, he returned to Odessa and the drug trade. Three years later he was tricked into selling a pound of heroin to federal agents in Eunice, New Mexico, but he avoided arrest by running into the desert and ultimately fleeing across the border to Ojinaga.

It was December 1976. A friend of Acosta's from prison, another U.S. citizen named Shorty Lopez, ran the drug concession in Ojinaga. Acosta fit in easily. Drawing on his contacts in Texas, he built an organization and began to move large quantities of marijuana across the river, paying Lopez the required percentage. Lopez was cocky and incautious, and did not last long. In 1977 he drove knowingly into an ambush and was gunned down. His replacement, chosen by general agreement among the traffickers, was a quieter man who had once studied for the priesthood. He lasted until December 1980, when U.S. authorities caught him at the Albuquerque airport and sent him to jail. By then Acosta was forty-three, and had a large mustache and a swarthy, deeply lined face. He was already the biggest operator in Ojinaga. He also seemed the shrewdest, and perhaps the most violent. No one was surprised when he emerged on top.

Acosta ruled for seven years, from early 1981 until the end of 1987. It was the most prosperous period in Ojinaga's history. Adventurers poured into the town from all over Mexico and the United States. The wealth was evident everywhere. Up in Marfa the ranching women wondered at the quality of the new boutiques in Ojinaga and believed they offered the most beautiful dresses this side of New York. In Presidio, gone were the days of selling used tractors and pumps. Rough-talking Mexicans entered the stores and peeled cash for thousand-dollar Stetsons, gold watches, and trunkloads of Cognac. As an air-taxi pilot, I ferried such men from Presidio to the airlines in El Paso and Odessa. They overpaid for the flights. They had manicured fingers. They wore diamond rings. The wonder was how they kept their lizard boots so clean.

Acosta was shipping marijuana by the ton. Authorities

in the United States counted five hundred members in his organization, not including hundreds more who worked under his umbrella, bought drugs from him, and paid the required percentage. Authorities in Mexico were equally aware of Acosta's achievements. They demanded and received protection payments of $100,000 a month. To show their appreciation, both the Mexican federal police and the army awarded Acosta credentials that effectively made him an agent of the government. His chief enforcer was similarly rewarded and once disappeared for a year, he claimed to Mexico City to work for Interpol. Acosta in turn recruited policemen and other officials in the small towns of Texas. He established contact with U.S. narcotics officers and handed over troublesome smugglers. Toward the end of his tenure he conspired with Customs to entrap his main rival in Chihuahua City. The plan fell through, but it illustrates the interdependence between traffickers and the law. When Acosta began to lose power, U.S. narcotics officers who were trying to work through him to get at his Colombian sources actually worried about his decline. In one of the more bizarre episodes, FBI agents fearful of Libyan terrorists sneaking into the United States traveled to Ojinaga to ask Acosta if he knew of any. He did not, but volunteered to fight them for free if they showed up. He pointed out correctly that he owed his success to the United States.

Acosta lived under constant threat of ambush. He moved under heavy guard and sometimes switched vehicles several times on a single trip across town. Tucked into his waistband was a .45 pistol, cocked and ready to shoot. In addition, he and his bodyguards carried military assault rifles. The weapons were not merely for show: Acosta's ferocity under fire helped him survive repeated attempts on his life. The gunfights were frenzied, drawn-out affairs fought in public. One lasted for about two hours and ranged throughout the town. Ojinaga had always known violence, but this was savagery of a completely new scale. In the bars and along the Rio Grande, countless men died in drug deals gone bad. Bystanders were hit in the crossfire. Several dozen men were killed in one feud alone that raged between Acosta and a rival trafficking family named Arevalo. The Arevalos had their own arrangement with Chihuahua City, and had never paid into the Ojinaga racket. Acosta wanted to change that and it cost him dearly. When he finally gunned down the Arevalo patriarch, the Mexican government issued a warrant for his arrest and he had to pay a million dollars to get off. By then a million dollars didn't mean much to him.

Acosta's most profitable business move was his introduction of Colombian cocaine to the established Ojinagan traffic. By 1985, long-range airplanes loaded with the coveted white powder started flying into Ojinaga directly from South America. In his biography of Acosta, *Druglord,* El Paso reporter Terrance Poppa describes the arrival of one such shipment, 1,800 pounds in approximately eight hundred one-kilogram (2.2-pound) bricks encased in wax. Acosta had the load buried in a subterranean tank beside a dirt runway, thirty miles southeast of Ojinaga. Several weeks later he had it brought to town. Poppa writes:

A platoon of Pablo's men dug back down to the tank hatch. Someone climbed into the tank and handed up the cocaine. The bricks were put into cardboard boxes in the back of two pickup trucks. This time, a squad of Mexican soldiers present to provide security escorted the shipment from the desert ranch to the outskirts of Ojinaga, where Pablo and a group of his pistoleros were waiting for the convoy alongside a dirt road. Following his custom, Pablo pulled a wad of bills from his shirt pocket and gave each of the soldiers a crisp twenty-dollar bill. They went back to Ojinaga independently.

Pablo's men drove the cocaine to a warehouse in Ojinaga on the Chihuahua highway, across the street from a gasoline station and a few blocks from Casa Chavez, where Pablo stored much of his pot.

This warehouse was inside a large lot enclosed by a high cement-block wall. The compound was strewn with propane tanks in the process of being modified and fitted with a smaller propane tank. . . . It was like a small factory, bustling with employees working overtime to meet a deadline.

Over the next few days the cocaine was broken down into seven separate loads, each packed inside one of the modified propane tanks. Once the tank was sealed with Bondo, it was bolted down to the floor of a pickup truck and hooked up to look like a functioning propane tank. A trusted runner drove the truck to Lomas de Arena or some other river ford, crossed the Rio Grande, and then drove it on to its destination.

In addition to selling and moving his own loads of cocaine, Acosta warehoused shipments for other traffickers along the entire border, from Tijuana to Matamoros. For this service alone he was paid at least a thousand dollars a kilogram, which means about a million dollars for a typical planeload. One or two airplanes arrived in Ojinaga every week. So cocaine was enormously profitable for Acosta. It was also his demise. He had been using it personally for some years, buying small quantities from friends in the United States and snorting or smoking it to keep going through the frantic work of smuggling. But now, with unlimited supplies available, he lost control of the habit. The other traffickers began to lose faith in him, as did his patrons in Chihuahua City.

But Acosta's greatest problem with cocaine was political. When U.S. narcotics agents discovered the quantities Acosta was moving, they met in El Paso and formed a "task force" to dismantle the distribution network and, if possible, to lure Acosta into the United States to be arrested. News of this leaked out, and newspapers in El Paso and Albuquerque published the first stories about Acosta. They portrayed him as a killer and one of the biggest drug traffickers in all of Mexico. Acosta was both flattered and concerned. Terrance Poppa approached Acosta through intermediaries and proposed an interview. Acosta agreed to it, perhaps to improve his image. The plan backfired. Poppa spent two days with Acosta in Ojinaga. His report, published as a series by the El Paso *Herald-Post* in December 1986, discussed the payments to Mexican officials and named names. The story was picked up by the wire services. The Mexicans did not appreciate this publicity. Two days later Mexico City gave orders for Acosta's arrest. This time it was for real: police jurisdiction over Ojinaga was suddenly switched from Chihuahua City to Juárez, and a new commander was flown in. Acosta fled. Four months later, in April 1987, he was found holed up in Santa Elena, his native village on the Rio Grande. With assistance from the FBI, Mexican agents flew by helicopter across Marfa and hit the village unexpectedly from the north. When Acosta shot back, they machine-gunned him to death.

Ojinaga confirms what Texans fear most about the border. Acosta's ghost lives in the faces of the swarthy men who walk its streets. The Anglo cowboys and the roughnecks from the oil fields who used to frequent the bars and whorehouses now stay away. The few who still visit go looking for trouble. Even the tourists, of whom there were never many, have gotten word. You may see an occasional German in search of the mythical West, or a Minnesotan stalking the winter sun. But Ojinaga is neither picturesque nor welcoming. My friends in Marfa urged me to leave by nightfall and to stop asking questions.

Visitors to Ojinaga are torn between the suspicion of evil and the obvious normalcy of life. Those who expect to find terror in the streets must leave disappointed. The Beiruts of the world are rare; more common strains of horror wear a placid expression. Knowing this, I walked again through the town, retracing the routes I had taken during Acosta's time. Fewer men displayed their guns—I saw none who were not uniformed.

But the uniforms were less reassuring than they would have been, say, in Europe. In Ojinaga the police agencies and the army are still openly involved in the narcotics traffic. In other ways, too, Ojinaga seemed unchanged.

Elegant houses still boasted their fenced and tended lawns, green against the dust of the streets. A scattering of neighborhood stores sold sparse inventories of canned goods and hardware. Crumbled adobe and broken glass littered the heart of town, where the buildings stood in stages of stalled construction and disrepair. People watched me warily, and kept their distance. I entered the Catholic church on one end of the central square and sat alone for an hour. The church was white and sparse, and bright with desert light streaming in through open doors. I listened to children playing on the street, the squeal of power steering, and the roar of a motorcycle circling the square, shifting gears. I thought the church looked unused. A woman finally came in holding the hand of a small boy, and stood with him before the large wooden Jesus. She prayed silently and wanted her son to do the same. The boy would have none of it. He squirmed, faced around, and tested the church's echoes. His mother held on to him grimly. She did not look hopeful about his future.

I went to visit Dr. Artemio Gallegos, an elderly physician who is the town's most prominent citizen. On the way to his clinic, I walked past the hulk of a van shattered by gunfire, in which the blood on the driver's seat had barely dried. Gallegos nodded heavily when I mentioned it to him; he had heard already and knew the story behind the assault, a matter of unpaid debts. Gallegos was something of an expert on gunshot wounds. We talked in his book-lined study, the scene of a deadly shoot-out in the 1970s. He took me next door to the examining rooms, and introduced me to a trafficker who had just killed a rival in a bar and had himself been shot in the head. The trafficker was a big man with a mustache and a lined face. He lifted his bandage to show me his wound and joked about the loss of his eye. A policeman laughed with him. I thought they seemed unusually cheerful.

Back in his study, I asked Gallegos about the town's past. He explained the history of the candelilla trade, and of Acosta, and after an hour he said, "You must understand the consequences of all this illegality. It is what has caused the town to grow. We learned to have a big tolerance for the narco-traffickers for a very simple reason—because they brought more money for everyone. But overall, I would say the quality of life went down. After Acosta, the government came in and wanted to clean up. Fine. We told them we needed clean drinking water. They told us to go to hell. Their 'cleanup' led only to depression, so by the time the traffickers returned, the town had learned to miss them."

He used the word *return* figuratively, since the traffickers had never actually left Ojinaga. For a few years they enjoyed quieter lives. But Ojinaga lies too close to the United States and is too accustomed to listening not to hear the call for narcotics.

The question of how much comes across here is nearly irrelevant. The entire border leaks. If you plug it in one place, you find that it leaks harder somewhere else. If you cripple one organization, you raise the market share for the others. If you kill one Acosta, you find whole populations waiting to take his place. Narcotics officers in the back country of West Texas understand this, and they take no solace from the fact that few arrests have been made since the death of Acosta. The situation is worse, not better. Ojinaga is leaking harder than ever before. Until he was sentenced to prison for smuggling cocaine, the traffickers even had an affectionate name for Sheriff Rick Thompson up in Marfa. They called him "La Puerta," which means "the door."

Other doors lie open from the Pacific to the Gulf of Mexico—in police departments, sheriffs' offices, and courthouses too numerous to know. Border Patrol guards quietly look the other way on their patrols and at their roadside checkpoints. Customs gatekeepers at the ports of entry are notorious for waving through narcotics by the carload. I talked to a group of smugglers at the Marfa jail who insisted that the corruption is as pervasive on the U.S. side as in Mexico. They exaggerated perhaps, but one federal official quietly told me he believed that fully half of the law enforcement officers along the Texas border are in the pay of the traffickers. Rick Thompson was an exception because he was flamboyant and famous, and because he was caught.

He was born in 1946, nine years after Pablo Acosta, and raised in Marathon, Texas, a desolate crossroads seventy miles east of Marfa. His father ran a gas station. While Acosta labored on the migrant trail, Thompson grew up strong and broad-shouldered, over six feet tall, with the rugged good looks of a movie actor. He had a reputation for brawling and for beating Mexicans. It was said he could go "either way," meaning break the law or abide by it. He graduated from high school in 1964, and joined the marines. The military made him a policeman and gave him a hint of the larger world. When he returned in 1967, he claimed to have served in Vietnam, the first of his public falsehoods. He attended the local college, got a job as a city cop in Marfa, and drove the Border Patrol bus that shuttled captured immigrants to the river. When in 1973 the old sheriff was gunned down outside of town, Thompson at the age of twenty-six was the natural choice for his replacement. The marines had already taught him not to slouch. The county supervisors appointed him to serve the remainder of a four-year term. Acosta was just getting out of prison.

It was a time when Texas lawmen stood for something. Years later I heard stories from neighboring towns of blacks thrown into jail, beaten, and fined for passing through. Soon after his arrival from New York, Donald Judd watched as a couple of deputies shook down an unfortunate longhair who had wandered into Marfa. They found an American flag in his trunk, and "because it touched the ground," they made him burn it. Judd described to me how the deputies stood in the highway, laughing as the longhair drove away. Judd himself was a longhair, but on the highest level. The deputies did not dare harass him, though he openly disapproved of Thompson.

Later Judd said to me, "But I never mistook Marfa for an artists' colony. I always wanted it to be a cow town." And it was.

By 1981, when Acosta took over the narcotics trade in Ojinaga, Thompson had survived the first stirrings of the Mexican mutiny and was confident in his rule over Presidio County. He had taken, in a cowboy way, to wearing fine clothes and expensive hats. He had few close friends, but the citizens voted for him anyway. When I asked about his power, another lawman said, "He was a big man and good-looking, you know. And he'd walk up to you on the street, grin down at you, put his hand on your shoulder, and say, 'Son, I've been meaning to talk to you. Why don't you stop by the office sometime.' And so you did. People just didn't say no to Rick Thompson."

Another old acquaintance said, "Come to think of it, he was always hustling. There was always an angle." Some angles were financial: Thompson got involved in a laundry and other small business ventures, none of which worked out. Other angles were political. Over the years, Thompson did a lot of favors, driving drunk ranchers home, breaking up fights, calming feuds, keeping people out of jail. Anglos called him the finest sheriff they had ever known, which was probably true. Mexicans called him "the great white hope," and quietly resented the selective nature of his justice, but they did not dare confront him.

In 1984 he campaigned on an antidrug platform, perhaps sincerely. His main concern was to keep the violence out of Presidio County. I think he admired Acosta. It is not clear whether they ever met, but they did send messages and reach accommodations, as one strong man to another.

In 1985, when Acosta was at the height of his powers, Thompson was elected president of the Texas Sheriffs' Association, a position that confirmed his greatness in his own eyes. People in Marfa said, "Rick's changed." He was more distant, less willing to do small favors. His arrogance suddenly seemed boundless. Unfortunately, at about the same time federal and state narcotics agents working along the border received orders to withdraw from local jurisdictions and redirect their efforts into coordinated operations against major drug traffickers. Thompson felt slighted. He reacted petulantly by cutting the federal agents out of further information in Presidio County, and in 1986 by forming his own eight-county narcotics "task force." Six years later, in 1992, he was still heading the task force when he was brought to justice for smuggling. Given his capacity for self-deception, he may not have seen this as a contradiction. The sentencing judge did.

Street gossip in Marfa had Thompson selling out to the traffickers as early as 1980, but no one talking really knew. It does seem likely that by the end of 1986, when Acosta was on the run, Thompson had entered the business. He was bitter and cynical, and felt he deserved better than the $20,000 sheriff's salary. His partner in the scheme was Robert Chambers, a mercenary, smuggler, and longtime associate of Acosta's. Chambers lived on his father's ranch near Candelaria, where he had grown up speaking fluent Spanish. Thompson had used him in the past for errands into Mexico and dirty work along the Rio Grande. In 1986 he was on probation for federal weapons violations. Thompson, who had access to the federal, state, and local police frequencies, kept Chambers posted on the whereabouts of other lawmen, allowing him to drive truckloads of marijuana safely north from the river. Eventually Thompson himself drove the loads, hundreds of pounds at a time in his official green Suburban, right through the Border Patrol checkpoint on the highway to Marfa. The country was still his, and he felt he could control the risk.

By 1990 federal narcotics officers knew of Thompson's association with Chambers and believed that the two of them were moving substantial quantities of drugs. The Customs agent in charge at Presidio said to me, "There was

enough smoke to mean fire. But we didn't have proof. We
had to be extra careful. Thompson was a politico and he
carried weight. He had stroke. He had power." Chambers,
on the other hand, was unprotected, and early in 1991 the
agents decided to go after him. Their break came in November of that year, when Chambers asked an old acquaintance to help with a special load. Thompson's grip
was slipping: he did not know that Chambers's acquaintance had become a federal informant. The load in question
was 2,400 pounds of cocaine due to cross the Rio Grande
in a few days. Chambers and the sheriff had been working
on the deal for almost a year. For transporting the load
away from the border they expected to split a million-
dollar fee.

The fee was a measure not only of the cocaine's value,
but also of its associated risks. Thompson may have suspected this. But by 1991 Hispanics had won every other
important office in Presidio County and seemed to be
gathering their strength to seize the sheriff's position in the
election of November 1992. History bore out the percep-
tion: after a few months of appointed service, Thompson's
gentle successor, Abe Gonzales, won the 1992 election
against an Anglo rancher by an overwhelming margin.
And Thompson was nothing if not an astute politician.
The cocaine deal was his chance to retire gracefully at the
age of forty-six.

The traffickers left Ojinaga in a convoy and moved the
cocaine upriver under the protection of a dozen Mexican
federal judicial police armed with rifles. People in the
villages they passed through would not have been surprised to see the police. Despite the anti-corruption efforts,
it is well known that no large shipments of narcotics can

move in northern Mexico without their involvement. Sometime after dark they came to San Antonio del Bravo, across from Candelaria, and drove a few miles farther upstream to the ford. It was December 2, 1991, a night of bitter cold on the Rio Grande. Chambers and his traitorous companion drove across the river, met the Mexicans, and began to shuttle the cocaine to a hiding place on Chambers's ranch. Thompson lurked nearby in his official Suburban, watching for trouble, talking to Chambers by radio. When Chambers's truck stalled, Thompson drove up out of the darkness and jump-started it. That was the least of his involvement. After the cocaine was safely hidden on Chambers's ranch, the sheriff loaded a third of it—about eight hundred pounds—into his Suburban, and drove it through Candelaria and on to Marfa, where he transferred it into the back of his horse trailer at the rodeo grounds. The next day he returned to the river and in two trips brought the rest of the load north.

The federal agents had stayed away to keep from spooking him, and they knew little of what had happened. On the night of December 3, their informant called to say that the deal had gone through. The agents staked out the rodeo grounds through a long cold night and at dawn seized the trailer. The cocaine lay under a loose covering of hay and nearly filled the two five-foot stalls. It was packaged into one-kilogram bricks, wrapped tightly in white plastic, and emblazoned with an emblem of a polo horse, which the agents took to be a trademark. The bricks in turn were packed into forty burlap sugar sacks.

Chambers was arrested later that day on his ranch near Candelaria. Realizing he had been betrayed, he agreed to testify against the sheriff. Word of Thompson's involvement spread rapidly. When federal agents interviewed him at his office, he looked worried and seemed older and smaller. He had three of his own lawmen in the room with him. When it was clear that the agents were not going to arrest him, he said, "Boys, let's not bullshit each other. I think from now on you're gonna have to go through my attorney."

The sheriff stonewalled. A week after Chambers's arrest he called a news conference and claimed that he had been running a sting operation, that the federal agents had blown it. The agents pointed out that even if this were true, he had no right to bring cocaine into the country without informing them.

Thompson tried to rally the ranchers to his side: he presented himself as a homespun hard-nosed sheriff, a good old boy being set up by an elitist federal bureaucracy. The line played well in Marfa, as it would throughout the rural West. It divided the Anglos into opposing camps of those who supported the sheriff and those who felt he had betrayed them. The emotion among the Hispanics was perhaps more realistic—a quiet trust that he had done himself in and would at last disappear from their lives.

After being indicted by a federal grand jury, Thompson was arrested on January 9, 1992, and held without bail away from Marfa in Pecos, Texas. And still he stuck to his story. He may have begun to believe it himself. Faced with Chambers's testimony, he pled guilty one month later to what he insisted was a federal technicality, "a little importation charge."

Thompson's political sense had apparently deserted him. From his jail cell in Pecos, he organized a letter writing campaign to influence the federal district judge,

Jerry Buchmeyer, who was to sentence him. Buchmeyer was unmoved, as were the citizens and lawmen who wrote letters condemning the sheriff for his treachery. Still, Thompson believed he would get a probated sentence. The U.S. attorney, living up to his part of the plea bargain, asked for only ten years. But on May 8, 1992, Judge Buchmeyer added up the points against Thompson and, in a three-hour proceeding, sentenced him to life in prison without parole. Thompson remained stoic throughout. His wife and young son wept.

Ojinaga weathered the storm easily. Acosta is a mythical memory, and now seems like the last of the small-time operators. The traffickers learned from his mistakes to keep a lower profile and to avoid the press. Despite the publicity surrounding Thompson's downfall, business on the river continued as usual. It is rumored that an additional five tons of cocaine were waiting to come across when Thompson was arrested, and that after a short delay, they did. This is perfectly believable. After Acosta's death, the reformer sent in by Mexico City was transferred, but the switch of police jurisdiction remained in force. It is perhaps no coincidence that the Ojinaga racket is said now to be run from Juárez, by someone with close ties to government.

Marfa has not fared so well. I asked an old friend there when he thought the town would recover from Thompson's fall and he answered, "Never." From a rancher's perspective it may be true. It is said that Thompson in prison is a changed man, and that he has grown long hair and a beard. He will never return. Marfa's last white hope is gone.

Nine

Far to the east, after hundreds of miles of virtual
wilderness, the border again is blighted by urban desperation. Before emptying into the Gulf of Mexico the
Rio Grande snakes across a semitropical coastal plain,
a green and hazy flatland known locally as the Lower
Valley. The north side, where 80 percent of the residents are Mexican-American, has long been weakened
by corruption and political bossism. *Colonias,* decrepit
farming towns, and three decayed cities—McAllen,
Harlingen, and Brownsville—attest to the lack of opportunity. Publicists there speak of a rich cultural heritage. No doubt. But as measured by income, health,
and education, the Lower Valley is among the poorest
regions in the United States. And to spite us all, it looks
like the future.

Across the river, Mexico is poorer still. Life is dominated by the presence of American manufacturers,
who have set up some of the border's largest *maquiladoras.* Reynosa, which lies on the Rio Grande, is a flat
industrial city of perhaps 300,000 people, about seventy

miles from the Gulf. To get there from Texas, you cross a big modern bridge, passing a mile of trucks waiting to clear Mexican customs, and an equally long line waiting to enter the United States. The trucks attest to the vigor of business and binational trade. Zenith alone employs ten thousand workers in Reynosa.

Colonia Roma is typical of the districts where they live. It sprawls across a swampy lowland beyond the Pemex refinery—a large and desolate slum, strewn with trash, where vegetation does not survive. The shacks are made of scraps discarded from the factories. Children wear rags and go barefoot. Here and there, a Coke sign hammered to a wall indicates a small grocery, a place perhaps with electric power. A paved road passes beside the neighborhood, on higher ground, and crawls with buses blowing smoke. During the shift changes at the *maquiladoras,* workers stream between the shacks and balance on planks across mud and sewage. The women dress in pressed skirts and blouses; they look like office workers from a better neighborhood in a better city. Many go into debt to achieve this effect. Inflation has outpaced wages in Mexico. The average *maquila* worker in Reynosa labors forty-five minutes for a quart of milk or a pound of chicken, two hours for a bottle of shampoo, three hours for two boxes of cornflakes or a toddler's used sweater, twenty hours for sneakers, and over a hundred hours for a double mattress.

Drainage in Colonia Roma is poor. The district flooded the week before I got there, and residents waited for the water to subside by perching with their belongings on their beds. This seemed hardly noteworthy to the family I went to see. Their yard was a mess of cinder-block rubble imbedded in mud. They lived in a single-room plywood house that was almost filled by two iron beds pushed together. On subsequent visits I counted eight people who slept there, but I may have missed a few. The oldest was a toothless Indian grandmother who questioned me about my religious beliefs. I was cautious: she wanted to talk about God's grace and the afterlife. The youngest resident was a girl, perhaps five, who seemed ill. One of the sons, who in his midtwenties had been working three years at Zenith, was small, thin, and discouraged.

I asked, "How is the job?"

He answered, "Good." But his eyes were furtive.

"Good?"

"Little good. The problem is there is no money."

"And the union?"

"It can't protect us."

"How long will you stay?" I asked.

"I don't think about it."

The shack smelled of lard and garbage. Smoke from a refuse fire drifted by the open door. Chairs hung from nails on the walls because there was no place for them on the floor. A pair of prized cowboy boots stood under the bed, by a stack of clothes. The kitchen consisted of a camp stove, a water jug, and an insulated box. There was a kerosene lantern, a transistor radio. The buzzing of flies mixed with the shouts outside.

Seen from a distance—say, in a photograph—such poverty evokes powerful feelings. Close up, however, it can seem unreal. It is bewildering that people you can touch, who share the air with you, can be suffering in conditions so different from your own. I have experienced this before in Africa, in the midst of starvation. We carry our own world with us and it is numbing.

It is an environmental future to be feared. When people live in cities built on industrial waste, they suffer. In the Lower Valley, miscarriage, birth defects, disease, and cancer rates are high. For this and the other calamities of their lives, the workers have begun to blame the United States. In Matamoros, the city of a half million that lies across the Rio Grande from Brownsville, Texas, I talked to a labor organizer named Maria Torres. She said, "Americans say they save us from starvation. But all of us who have come to the north, if we had stayed where we were, we would not be dying of hunger. Here on the border, we are just slaves."

That word *slave* kept reappearing. Upriver I had seen graffiti scrawled defiantly across a bridge: NO SOMOS ESCLAVOS! "We are not slaves!" And in Reynosa's Colonia Roma, I had talked to a man whose greatest wish was for his children to work in the *maquiladoras*. He said, "In the past we were nothing but the slaves of the rich. And if we are still slaves today, at least the *maquiladoras* pay us more."

I quoted him to Torres. She became calmer and said, "No one is against the plants. No one wants to close them down. We ask only for better conditions and we are willing to compromise. But we refuse absolutely to be used as a dumping ground for industrial wastes. The president of Mexico claims he won't allow contamination. He claims environmental enforcement will be part of free trade. But why should we believe him? We've seen what they do: they close down the companies that contaminate the least and they leave the big polluters alone." She named them for me and said, "There are strong interests involved. The neighborhoods around the plants have denounced them, but nothing is done."

In Matamoros the best-known case of this occurred around a chemical plant called Chemica Flor, which sits by a mountain of its own waste. The plant, partly owned by DuPont, produces hydrogen fluoride, a volatile, toxic, and highly corrosive acid shipped to the United States for use in the manufacture of Teflon coatings. The risks of having such a facility within the bounds of a city are considerable. When nearby residents objected, Mexican authorities ordered the permanent evacuation of neighborhoods within two kilometers (1.25 miles) of the stacks: ten thousand people were affected. The residents marched in protest. Finally the authorities "backed down" and allowed the people to remain. Such false concessions have sustained the Mexican government for decades. But the technique has limits.

Across town, I visited a General Motors facility that makes bumpers. The buildings were big, square, and anonymous. They had nice little lawns. I arrived during the shift change, when several thousand workers—again mostly young women—streamed out and climbed onto the colorful buses waiting to take them back to their shacks. I went around the side of the main building, to the ditch into which the plant's outflow pipes drain. Activists from the United States have taken samples here showing massive levels of xylenes, ethyl benzene, acetone, toluene, and methylene chloride. I did not need a test tube—from a hundred yards away I could smell the solvents. They dribbled from the outflow pipes in paint-colored water and floated off through the city in the ditch.

Senior General Motors spokesmen have denied this condition, and in all sincerity. The corporation does not intend to pollute. Workers are provided with tanks into which to purge their paint guns. But to save time, they simply purge the guns into the drains, which empty into the ditch. Mexico has adopted strict laws regulating toxic wastes, but government technicians measure the outflow water only for feces and bacteria. In addition, Mexican laboratories are notorious for falsifying results. So for a variety of reasons, the industrial chemicals do not officially exist. If they did, nothing would be done anyway. General Motors' Mexican landlords were legally obligated to build a treatment plant, if not for chemicals, at least for sewage. Instead they dug the ditch. This was not unusual. General Motors' ditch empties into a larger flow, the central canal, where it mixes with untreated municipal sewage and the poisonous outflow from an entire city of unchecked industry.

I spoke to a chemist in Brownsville, who said, "G.M.'s problem is they empty directly into a ditch. Other plants empty into pipes, which empty into other pipes, which empty into the main canal. It's practically impossible to trace their spills." Speaking of *maquiladoras* in general, he said, "The companies hide in their own corporate structures. They pass responsibility upward. If they go high enough, they can find people who don't know what's going on. They don't have to lie."

The central canal in Matamoros flows through residential neighborhoods. When residents complained, Mexican federal cleanup money was used to cap it for a mile or two and hide it from view. The covering was made in part of rock and gravel, which was later discovered to be toxic waste. A string of playgrounds was built on it. Word got out and the playgrounds lie unused. The canal does not empty into the Rio Grande. The discharge emerges from the city, flows southeast, and twenty miles below the border feeds into the Gulf of Mexico, where fish swim it north again.

The fear of poisoning is not an abstraction. Industrial accidents in Matamoros have sent hundreds of people to the hospital and forced thousands of others to evacuate their houses. On the night of December 6, 1990, a tank in the center of town overheated, blew a valve, and leaked a cloud of toxic vapor. The vapor entered the ventilation system of another *maquiladora*, a manufacturer of electric blankets, about three blocks away, and sent fifty women to the hospital. Slowly dissipating, it drifted over the Rio Grande into Brownsville, where the stench caused terror in the streets.

Maria Torres, the labor organizer, took me to a neighborhood sandwiched between two chemical plants: one brewed pesticides, the other detergents. By the standards of Matamoros, the neighborhood was middle class. The houses were made of rough, unpainted wood, but they had electricity, running water, and small yards. Most of the families had moved there in the 1930s, when cotton dust was the biggest nuisance.

A chemical smell wafted through the area and burned softly in my throat. The day was hot and I had a headache.

A stout woman with crooked teeth, a friend of Torres's, invited us into her house. We sat on chairs covered in padded red vinyl in a room the size of a closet. Through a doorway veiled by a beaded curtain I heard a television. An open fuse box was fixed to the wall, and a Coors-shaded light hung from the ceiling. A new telephone stood on a cabinet.

The woman offered me a glass of water and I declined. I asked her if she worried about the chemicals next door. She said, yes, ever since the explosion of 1983, when a pipe had burst at the insecticide plant and sprayed poisonous foam over the houses. I asked her to describe it. She said, "It snowed foam. We were afraid and ran with the children, thinking only of saving ourselves. Where we touched the foam, we got sores on our feet. The next day it rained, and the poison spread through the neighborhood. We were kept out for eight days. Our clothes were contaminated and destroyed. We had to kill our animals. Pigs, chickens, dogs, cats. We had seven ducks. They were all buried in a trench in the company compound."

I wandered across the street and talked to an old man who told me of digging holes and smelling chemicals in the groundwater, which lies close below the surface. The detergent factory had built evaporation ponds next to his house. When they overflowed, his chickens picked at the water and died. Chickens in Matamoros are like canaries in a mine—but here when the canaries die the miners stay on.

Later, Torres took me for a walk along a ditch where discharges from bordering plants sink into the soil. The water was black and it turned milky when I tossed rocks into it. Families live there along the railroad tracks, in a district called *Chorizo* because it is long and narrow like a sausage. They drink from tainted wells and hang their clothes to dry on the fences that separate them from industry. The border is full of these fences without effect.

Maria Torres, who wanted so for me to see her industrial nightmare, is a woman well known to the poor of Matamoros. Her full name is Maria Torres Guadalupe Martinez. I first met her at a café at the heart of the city to talk about her efforts to organize women workers in the *maquiladoras*. At forty-eight, she has a gentle face coarsened by hardship. For most of her adult life she worked on the production lines in Matamoros for a company called Kemet, which manufactures capacitors. Now she works for an organization called *Comite Fronteriza de Obreras,* or the Border Committee of Working Women. The committee collects no dues and has no membership rolls, but is well known to thousands of *maquila* workers along the lower Rio Grande. Its approach is low-key: it does not exhort the women to march or strike, but rather encourages them to meet discreetly in small groups in the shantytowns. They teach themselves about their rights under Mexican federal labor law and about the occupational dangers in the factories. Torres helps them to learn, as she herself learned. She encourages them to ask for small improvements from the *maquila* managers and better representation from the huge Mexican union, the CTM. Faced in their offices with delegations of women who are calm and resolute, the managers and union men sometimes give in to the demands. As a result, wages and working conditions in Matamoros are slightly better than elsewhere on the border. Torres has nourished herself with these small victories. She is a strong woman who has grown stronger with age.

I heard she went to Mexico City with a coalition of Mexican and American union men concerned about the effects of free trade. They met with scholars in a conference room at the *Collegio de Mexico*. Someone gave a presentation. The discussion that followed was too theoretical for Torres's taste. She butted in and said in Spanish, "What I want to talk about is not free trade. What I want to talk about is, I worked eighteen years in the *maquiladoras*. I washed parts in methylene chloride with my bare hands. No one told me it was poisonous. No one gave me safety equipment." Looking annoyed at the interruption, some of the academics pushed back from the conference table. Torres persisted. She had brought along the label from a spool of lead solder, and because it was in English, she asked an American to read it: CONTAINS LEAD WHICH MAY BE HARMFUL TO YOUR HEALTH. LEAD IS KNOWN TO CAUSE BIRTH DEFECTS OR OTHER REPRODUCTIVE HARM. FEDERAL AND STATE LAWS PROHIBIT THE USE OF LEAD SOLDER IN MAKING JOINTS IN ANY PRIVATE OR PUBLIC POTABLE (DRINKING) WATER SUPPLY SYSTEM. AVOID BREATHING FLUX FUMES EMITTED DURING SOLDERING. FLUX FUMES MAY CAUSE PULMONARY IRRITATION OR DAMAGE. AFTER HANDLING SOLDER, WASH HANDS WITH SOAP AND WATER BEFORE EATING OR SMOKING. Torres said, "There are thousands of women handling solder who have no idea what this warning says. They are told nothing."

When I met her in Matamoros she continued the story. "They don't have time before lunch to wash. They eat greasy tacos, which become black from their hands." She spoke from experience, the source of her power.

Torres was born in 1944 in Cardenas, a large town in the state of San Luis Potosí, about 250 miles south of the border. Her father was a railroad laborer who died by falling off a train when she was a baby. Her mother went to work as a domestic for other railroad families. They could not afford to pay but provided food and a place for the night. Maria Guadalupe grew up in their shacks, sleeping in blankets on the floor. When she was seven she caught typhoid and nearly died. She spent a year recovering. At the age of ten, having completed the third grade, she gave up on school and went to work with her mother.

I asked about their relationship. She said, "I used to get angry with her because she was authoritarian. But she gave me a lot of love over the years. When I was sick with typhoid, when I had nightmares, I often woke up in her arms."

Her mother dreamed of working in the United States. "When I was eleven, she left me with my godmother and went north to the border to pick cotton. She didn't cross, but she came close. I was very lonely. My godmother had a beauty shop that catered to prostitutes. She made me work hard cleaning, building the wood fires, making tortillas. She beat me. When my mother returned, she promised we would never be separated again.

"The first time I left Cardenas, I was fourteen. We moved to Tampico and worked in homes there, but we suffered a lot. My mother went to one house, and I went to another, and during the week we didn't see each other. My mother came on Sundays and left her earnings with

223

me. I worked for my keep. I had a windowless room. There were alley cats who screeched and frightened me."

Sitting at the table in the Matamoros café, she began to cry. I waited for her. She apologized and said, "These are things I have never talked about. I had one box with my clothes. The people in Tampico got into it and robbed our money." She cried some more.

After she composed herself, she said, "Then someone gave us an address and we moved to Mexico City. It was very emotional for me—I had always wanted to see Mexico City.

"My mother kept house for the wife of a doctor and the doctor gave me work in a pharmaceutical lab. My first assignment was to wash the vials, but soon I was taught more interesting jobs. I felt guilty when I got promoted over others, but I loved the work because it related to medicine. One of the chemists went on vacation and I was given his responsibilities. I filled orders for penicillin and other medicines. I had no supervisor. I had the keys, and opened and closed the department. But my mother still had the dream of crossing into Texas and we came here to the border, to Matamoros, when I was sixteen."

It was 1960. The Bracero guestworker program was still in full swing. Mexicans could cross the bridge into Brownsville without documents; it was thought of as part of the natural border traffic. Nonetheless, moving to the United States was a big step. Mother and daughter hesitated for eight months in Matamoros, working in the upper-class neighborhood.

When finally they ventured into Brownsville, they quickly found live-in jobs. Torres became the nanny of four children, for eight dollars a week. She stayed three years, until she was twenty, saved a little money, and went often to the dances. Then she and her mother moved to Harlingen, the next town north, where again they found jobs in separate households. Harlingen lasted a year, until someone called the Border Patrol. When the agents came, Torres ran into the fields and hid in a furrow. Afterward, her employers drove her back to Brownsville, where her mother, too, had taken refuge.

By then you needed a Border Crossing Card to take the bridge. The women had a friend in Mexico who was sleeping with someone in American Immigration, who got them the card. They found work in Brownsville. Torres wanted to return to Mexico; her mother did not. They argued about it.

I asked Torres why she wanted to return. She said, "I felt alone in the United States and this loneliness was overwhelming me. And then, a lot of things happened in the families I did not like. The parents didn't give enough time to their children, they were so busy with other things. I didn't want to be part of it."

I said, "So you disapproved."

"The young had too much liberty, and did not use it well. I don't mean they should have been saints, but they needed to think more about the future. When they got older they threw parties in their bedrooms. One girl told me, 'My body is my own and I can do what I want with it.'"

I shrugged. "My impression is that Mexican women—for instance, the *maquila* workers—are promiscuous, too. Look at all the unwed mothers."

She blamed it on the border. "Industrialization is destroying our families. They work in shifts and hardly see each other. The women get the jobs and the men are forced to be idle. This is very difficult on them. The man from the interior is used to being the moneymaker. To depend on a woman is degrading."

"Some women would say it's about time."

"But the Mexican man has been raised a different way. It does no one any good to destroy him."

She had other complaints about the border culture. "We want to copy the United States and we copy things we shouldn't. When Americans cross the bridge, their behavior changes. During spring break, college students come down here, swearing and shouting and drinking beer on the streets—things we may not do. They litter, though they would not in their own country. This influences us."

One Saturday when she was in her midtwenties, Torres crossed the bridge from Brownsville and rented a room in an old house on Morelos Street, in the central district of Matamoros. Her mother did not approve of the expense. Torres bought the basics: a bed, a two-burner stove and a tank of gas, a frying pan, two cups, and two plates. Her mother stayed with her for the weekend, but returned on Monday to Brownsville. That morning, Torres went to the union office looking for a job.

It took two months to get one, at a pottery factory. After the first week she learned she would not be paid because she was "in training." She wondered how she was going to survive. There were twenty workers there, and they told her this was standard. She answered, "If they haven't paid you either, then you should ask for your money."

226

They told her not to make trouble.

When the owner arrived, she said to him, "I won't work here anymore, but you owe me for the work I've already done." She pointed to the pots she had made. "I did all this, and I'm sure you'll sell it. I won't leave until you pay me."

The owner refused.

Torres raised her voice. Using strong language, she said, "These other women have been here for months, and have never been paid for their training either. You owe them, too."

The owner hushed her and agreed to pay. He wanted to write her a check, but she had never in her life been to a bank and she demanded cash. Leaving the factory, she waved the money at the other workers and cried, "Look! Look!" She heard later that they, too, were paid.

The next factory was a clandestine operation making knitted handbags. There were twelve workers. They had no chairs or tables, but sat on newspapers on the floor. One day a union man arrived and got into a shouting match with the owner, who was Italian. The union man took out a pistol and made the owner pay the workers then and there. Then he said, "Any who want to work in an electronics factory, come with me in my car." The car was a black Buick. Torres was the first one in. The others crowded in after her, until the union man barely had room to steer. Somehow he drove them to his office.

The electronics factory was an American *maquiladora*, set up by the Electronic Control Corporation to manufacture electrical coils. The union was supplying the workers. There were two hundred. Torres was given a three-month probationary contract with a promise of permanent employment if she performed well.

At the café in Matamoros she showed me what the job entailed: she folded a paper napkin and with deft and reflexive fingers simulated wrapping wire around a spool. The company required the women to produce two boxes of four hundred coils a day, six days a week, for about eighteen cents an hour. Despite swollen and bloody hands, Torres caught on quickly, and by her second week was producing four boxes a day. The supervisors were pleased, but after eight months the company still had not given her a permanent position. Then, just before Christmas and the mandatory two-week bonus, all two hundred workers were fired.

Torres was in trouble. Her savings were gone, and her clothes, which she had been given while working as a nanny, were wearing out. Her mother moved in with her to help with the rent, and both women took occasional day jobs in Brownsville. But Torres was determined to stay in Mexico. Every morning she walked to the union hall. Another eight months went by. She knew already about the difficult conditions at Kemet, the *maquiladora* where she was to work for eighteen years. She took the job there because she felt she had no choice. It was 1969 and she was twenty-five.

Kemet was as bad as they said. She worked in the department of injection molding, forming capacitor bodies from hardening epoxy. She washed the bodies bare-handed in methylene chloride, a volatile solvent that turned her skin papery and white. Methylene chloride is a chlorinated hydrocarbon, linked to liver damage, birth defects, and cancer. It is in the same chemical family as chloroform and it can have similar soporific effects. The warning labels cautioned in English against breathing the fumes and mentioned narcosis, respiratory failure, and death. The workers did not understand the dangers. Their supervisors probably did not, either.

They were all under constant pressure to increase their production. "Once they brought in a man who stood beside us, watching the clock, and wouldn't let us go to the bathroom. Every hour he came by with a file to check the production. Many women felt it necessary to work right through the breaks. He told us not to talk. If we looked up, he ordered us to work."

I asked what his orders sounded like.

"With just a glance, he ordered us." She laughed. "He wanted us to sit there like statues. I rebelled by talking, by singing, by getting others to sing. If he accelerated the belt, I loaded it up with too many units so they would fall off. Sometimes I sabotaged the machine, and while the mechanics tried to fix it, I took a rest."

I asked, "What happened in the end?"

Her answer surprised me. "Eventually the man relaxed. He became our friend. When he had to leave he threw a party for us. That was before I knew about my rights."

I asked, "And now, would he still be your friend?"

She smiled. "Probably not."

She was never a docile employee, and over time she grew angry. "I felt they were constantly loading more work on us. I began to ask the others, 'Don't we have any rights?' One day my friend Ludivina told me her brother, who was a law student, had mentioned a federal labor law to her. This was the first I heard of it."

By then Torres had put in eleven years at Kemet. The

idea of a comprehensive labor law, its mere existence, strengthened her resistance to the supervisors. But she did not know where to find this law or how to use it. She kept asking questions. Eventually she discovered that an American was coming from across the river and holding meetings in a Matamoros church, teaching Mexican workers about their rights. The American was Ed Krueger, then fifty, a soft-spoken man who had spent years helping the migrant farm laborers of Oklahoma and Texas. In February 1981, Torres went to her first meeting and took fifteen Kemet women with her.

The rest of the story—her success as an organizer—I knew already. I asked her about the American managers at Kemet and their attitudes toward safety. She was not unfair. "One day they announced everyone would have to wear safety glasses. That was it—no explanation. The girls complained about having to wear something that wasn't natural to them. The glasses didn't fit and they gave a slight magnification even for girls who didn't need it. The managers answered, 'Just wear them.' By then I was on the health and safety committee. After the first month we asked for more educational material. The managers finally brought in a movie that showed a wire sticking in a woman's eye. It was dramatic because the eye was bleeding. When the workers saw that, they finally accepted the safety glasses."

I asked her to generalize. "Do you think the managers are reckless?"

"They worry most about losing time. They don't pressure the supervisors to enforce the safety procedures, because everyone knows the procedures slow the production line."

We had been sitting in the café for most of the day. She said she still lived with her mother but no longer in the rented room in central Matamoros. She smiled. "It was unlivable. The house was so rotten that a man upstairs fell through the floor and landed in the bed of a woman below. He was walking from one room to another. Luckily, she had just rolled over. In the rain, we had to put our furniture on blocks; in hurricanes, we had to leave altogether. I went to the union and the federal housing authority, but no one would help. This went on for three years and our situation kept getting worse."

In frustration she wrote a letter to the president, Miguel de la Madrid, complaining that the government did not care about the people. Three months later she got a letter back. She took it to the chief housing official, who was surprised and asked her to wait. She did nervously, thinking he would trick her. But the man returned and said, "For me, this is an order." He took out a map that showed new houses, and invited her to choose one. Torres by then was involved in the workers' rights movement, and she knew how to handle herself. She said, "Look, I want a good house with good plumbing. And I don't want a lot of neighbors—I need a sense of privacy. And I want to live close to a school, so when I get old I can at least sell gum."

She chose a cinder-block house toward the edge of town. It had a living room, a kitchen, and two small bedrooms— just right for a middle-aged woman and her elderly mother. After years of difficulty, the leaking roof seemed like the smallest inconvenience.

Ed Krueger drove me skillfully in his old Mazda station wagon through the wheel-deep mud of a Reynosa shantytown. Krueger is the quiet midwesterner who introduced Maria Torres to her rights and who stands in the shadows behind the effort to organize *maquila* workers. As Mexican industrialization proceeds, history may show his importance.

You would never know it by looking at him. Now sixty-three, Krueger has a kind face and modest bearing, and speaks so softly that at times he is hard to hear. Under the rattling of the car, he said, "I used to get stuck more often. I was born in Indiana, in a town called Wakarusa, which means 'knee deep in mud.' Sometimes it seems like I'm still there." He smiled gently, as if to apologize for talking about himself. But that was our agreement: six months after meeting him, I had overcome his philosophical reluctance and returned to ask about his history. I knew this about him already: he lives just north of the border, in Edinburg, Texas. Like Roberto Martínez in San Diego, he is employed by the American Friends Service Committee, the Quakers, and must survive on the smallest of salaries. His wife is a Mexican-American from the Lower Valley who works as an immigrant rights advocate. They have a small house. Their son attends Harvard on a scholarship.

I also knew that Krueger had proved to be an extremely effective political organizer. I thought of him as a professional subversive. He laughed when I told him this, but he guessed it was a fair description. He has worked most of his life to subvert the existing order, first among the small towns of Texas and now south of the Rio Grande, among the *maquiladoras*. The factory managers know it too, and for a while they succeeded in keeping him out of Reynosa. A local newspaper called him a mole and published his home phone number. He got threatening calls. Photographs of him were posted in the Zenith guardhouses. The Reynosa police warned him to stay away. Typically, it was the official union, the CTM, that feared him most. The irony of all this, as I pointed out to Krueger, is that in the long run by organizing the workers he could perhaps save the union and the factories from themselves.

The shantytown called Lucio Blanco floated in a sea of mud to the horizons. Krueger slithered to a stop for a hen and her chicks. He got out of the car and shooed them to safety, stepping awkwardly in the mud. People in the shacks watched. He smiled broadly at them, waved, and said, *"Buenos dias, buenos dias!"* They did not answer. He got back in the car. As we drove on, he began to talk about his work. He said, "It's important to work in several different areas at once, partly for my own emotions. That way if things aren't going well somewhere, they might be going well somewhere else." In other words, though he was having to start over again here in Reynosa, downriver in Matamoros his efforts had paid off. About Matamoros, Krueger said, "The women have forced even the union to take their side. The educational process has been going on long enough there that even with all the new workers coming into the city most people are getting counseled on their rights. You can see the difference that makes. It spreads from the factories all through town. There is a greater sense of hope and dignity, a self-confidence that comes from doing things on their own. Now even the *colonias* are organized. Despite the competing organizations, the people are working together. The houses and the lots around them reflect their self-esteem. And there's no doubt that their wages lend dignity to their lives. They're finally making ten dollars a day versus half that here in Reynosa."

He lapsed into thoughtful silence. We passed a cluster of uniform shacks, twelve by twelve feet, made of composition wood. They were run-down and had yards littered with garbage. Krueger said, "Self-esteem is obviously a big problem in Reynosa. These houses were put in here by an ecumenical group, the 'World Servants.' It was the typical Christmas basket approach. I wonder where they are now. Church people seem to feel they can go in with a few million dollars and fix up the *colonias*. But it never works. You would expect churches to think more deeply, wouldn't you? There has to be a spirit of community before you start plopping down structures. People in Reynosa need to act for themselves. If you help the factory workers in the *colonias* get a reasonable salary, they will use that money effectively. Of course from the churches' point of view, the advantage of putting up structures is that it is ideologically neutral."

A slow rain fell. We parked by a one-room plywood shack with a neatly fenced yard and outhouse. The young woman who lived there, whose name was Olga, had recently gone to work for the committee as a labor organizer. Krueger had given her the initial training; he had returned now to encourage and advise her. She greeted us warmly, and invited us in out of the rain. We left our muddy shoes at the door. The house had a concrete floor,

two wooden chairs, a half table, a convertible sofa, a propane stove, and a television hooked to a car battery. The
rain pattered on the roof, which did not leak. Despite its
cleanliness, the house smelled vaguely of sewage.

Olga had been fired from a General Motors plant after
standing up at a union meeting and asking why the workers' dues seemed to disappear. A friend told her about the
committee and introduced her to Krueger. Now she
showed him a list of *maquila* workers who might be interested in coming to a meeting. The list was short. Olga had
encountered apathy, suspicion, and fear, and was embarrassed by her lack of progress. She deferred to Krueger as
one might to a boss. He did not want this. He urged her
not to rush things, and reminded her to let the workers
come to her. He gave her sheets to hand out—some in
cartoon form—on workplace hygiene, domestic violence,
and the federal labor law. He consulted a small black
agenda crowded with appointments, and arranged to return in five days. He mentioned that she might ask some
of the more interested women to meet with him then. He
reminded her that they would have nothing to fear here
in the shanty town, far from the factories.

After we drove away, he said of Olga, "We have to be
very careful. The people we work with have had more
than enough failure. Our most constant problem is their
feeling of defeat. We don't want them to feel defeated in
this, too."

Krueger tries to work himself out of the job. "I don't
have a big staff, so people realize from the start that they
aren't going to be able to depend on some strong leader to
rescue them. People reach a point in their understanding

when they want to guide themselves. And it does become a movement. Sometimes it's just an assembly line of workers. Or it might be factorywide. Or it might be a whole city.

"After groups develop independently, you can bring people together for meetings, and they find great joy and a cross-fertilization of thought. The excitement that comes from sharing what they've been through gives them hope and a real sense of strength. I can see that happening someday between Matamoros and Reynosa. If only 5 percent of the people participate in the meetings, they will educate the others. There's no denying the multiplier effect."

Krueger spoke from years of experience in the service of the poor. His father was a minister of the Evangelical and Reformed Church. "Not a fundamentalist, and not an intellectual, but concerned about people and their dignity, and justice. That was my inheritance, a sense of love and forgiveness." Krueger's mother was a woman of midwestern stock, devoted to gardening, cooking, and her five children. They lived a closed and protected life: Krueger was twelve before he met someone who had been divorced, and he still remembers the shock. The family moved from Indiana to Kansas to central Texas. Krueger attended Elmhurst College, a church-school near Chicago, where in 1952 he earned a degree in Spanish and sociology. He spent two summers in Mexico, working with the Quakers on a reforestation project, and decided then that he would devote himself to helping others. He enrolled in the Missouri seminary of what was to become the United Church of Christ, spent a year in agricultural school, and dropped out to work with the Migrant Ministry, traveling with the farmworkers through Texas and the Midwest. Many of the farmworkers came from the Lower Valley.

I asked if he proselytized them and he smiled. "Never. But we did try to 'enrich the faith of the people.' "

I asked how. He said, mostly by setting an example. He taught English and sanitation, and arranged for doctors and nurses to visit the camps. After several years he returned to the seminary, and in 1958 he was ordained as a minister of the United Church of Christ, and sent as a missionary to rural Honduras. There he observed that people's faith had stagnated near the main mission station, where the missionaries directed the religious activities, but that in the mountain villages, which escaped close supervision, the chapels maintained by the converts themselves were filling to capacity.

I admitted to Krueger my lack of enthusiasm for this type of success.

He answered, "I went there as a beggar who had found food, and I shared it with others who were also beggars and were looking for food."

"Why give them one kind of potato when they've got another?"

"What I saw in Honduras was a system of belief and superstition that seemed oppressive, that took away people's freedom."

"Anthropologists might call you ethnocentric."

"They might." He laughed. "But a missionary can come not in judgment, but in sharing, without trying to impose."

Krueger, the political operative, still saw himself in

237

some way as a missionary—although he never spoke to *maquila* workers of God.

After leaving Honduras in 1961, he returned to the Migrant Ministry in southwestern Oklahoma. Once a year he met in a cheap California motel with a eight other social activists seeking alternatives to the Christmas basket approach. They agreed that political education and group power was the solution, and together they plotted strategies to nurture people's self-confidence. Eventually Krueger left Oklahoma, and by following the migrants' trail backward came to the source of their misery, the Lower Valley.

In 1967 he was hired by the Texas Council of Churches as a social worker, and he began to organize neighborhood committees among the rural *colonias* north of the Rio Grande, applying the techniques devised in the California motel. Then came the strike.

Demanding a pay raise from thirty-five cents to fifty cents an hour, the workers at a big celery and cantaloupe operation called La Casita walked off the job during the harvest. The strike spread to other farms. Activists from Cesar Chavez's United Farm Workers arrived, as did the police and more than twenty Texas Rangers.

On the night of May 26, the strikers organized a picket line where the railroad crossed Main Street in the poor river town called Mission, Texas. By the time Krueger got there, several dozen farmworkers had been arrested. Krueger walked up to the Rangers' captain—who had a hat, cigar, belly, and boots—and asked him where the farmworkers had been taken. The captain snarled, "Krueger, you're masterminding this whole thing."

The situation seemed under control. The night was cooling. One of the strikers arrived with hamburgers. Just then a train came through, blocking the view of an Associated Press photographer standing on the far side of the tracks. The Rangers moved in fast. Krueger saw the captain knock the hamburgers to the ground. He turned on Krueger and threw him to another ranger, who held his face within inches of the passing train. Krueger was frightened and held very still. The train passed and the AP photographer began snapping pictures. The Rangers shoved Krueger into the back of a patrol car, crowded in with him, and drove off into the night. One of them turned from the front seat and said, "Krueger, you're no preacher, you're just a troublemaker."

Krueger said, "God bless."

The ranger, perhaps thinking Krueger had spoken facetiously, slapped him hard in the face. It was a dangerous moment. The car sped along country roads at over a hundred miles an hour. A sharp curve approached. Krueger saw it, but was silent. The other rangers got the driver to slow. That calmed all of them.

Krueger was booked in Edinburg for unlawful assembly, and he spent twenty-four hours in jail. While he was there, he asked the police rhetorically why they wanted to stop the farmworkers' movement. Of course he already knew the answer in its full complexity. It was 1967 and a difficult time for many Americans.

The strike failed and the farmworkers returned to work without a contract. But under Krueger's guidance, the *colonias* organized and began to press for political power. For Krueger himself, the arrest was unfortunate since it thrust public attention on him. The idea of a white Protestant working among the *colonias* frightened the traditionalist Anglo community. It was said that Krueger was "messing with the Mexicans" and "organizing" cells. Embarrassed, the Texas Council of Churches fired him in 1969. He vowed never again to wander into public view.

That was the year Crystal City revolted, man landed on the moon, Richard Nixon was president, and Ed Krueger was thirty-nine. His old friends at the United Church of Christ gave him employment, and the freedom to work in Beeville, an east Texas town that was 70 percent Mexican-American and sorely in need of subversion. Krueger made up his mind to go there after he heard that the schools provided no lunches to the students. Not surprisingly, he discovered a local government dominated by an Anglo elite. He walked the barrios on the west side of town with a survey form to find out what the residents knew about city hall, the county courthouse, the school board. He met with blank stares. The residents did not even know they should care. The east side of town, where the Anglos lived, might have lain across an international boundary.

Krueger started holding meetings on Friday evenings at a concrete table in a west side park. At first only a handful of elderly people attended. But slowly the crowd grew. Krueger asked a few people to go to the courthouse to sit in on the county commission meetings. They were humiliated there, and returned to talk of their indignation. The west side began to grumble.

Krueger fed the discontent with a one-page weekly newsletter, written in Spanish and English, in which he reported on the doings of local government. Once, without giving it much thought, he noted that the city council had decided to change the west-side street names to those of the east side. To his surprise, the crowd at the park meeting swelled.

Krueger rushed to the library, documented the fact that there were three to four times as many residences on the west side as on the east side, and passed the information on to a voluble Hispanic grocer. The grocer talked to his friends and customers. Krueger stayed away. At the next city council meeting eighty-five Mexican-Americans from the west side showed up to object to the name changes. Shocked and confused, the city council backed down.

For the west side, it was an important victory. For Krueger, still concerned about the lack of school lunches, it was a lesson in allowing people to set their own agendas. The meetings continued to grow. People began complaining about the unpaved streets and the lack of streetlights.

Krueger said, "Also, they became aware of filing deadlines for elections."

"How?" I asked. "Did you tell them?"

"Well . . . yes."

A year after his arrival, the Mexican-Americans won control of the city government and the school board. They raised the taxes and instituted school lunches. Krueger, the man in the shadows, began withdrawing.

To me he said, "The best part was that my name never got in the newspaper. I could even go to eat on the east side of town. The Anglos saw me around, but they didn't know who I was." He smiled. "Sometimes you can use segregation to your advantage."

As you can use the Rio Grande.

After Beeville Krueger tried to organize a similar town nearby, but could never move the people past their apathy. He managed to get them food stamps, a type of "emergency work" too close to the Christmas basket to satisfy him. He moved to Bakersfield, California, and worked for a while with the United Farm Workers, but found to his regret that the union had grown autocratic and had lost track of its original purpose. The experience reinforced his distrust of conventional hierarchies, and reminded him once again of the danger of strong leadership. He returned to the Lower Valley and, with no other source of income, went to work picking crops.

In 1975, the American Friends Service Committee sent him to southern Chile to give technical farming assistance to Indian communities. When he came home three years later, he discovered the difficult conditions in the big new assembly plants across the Rio Grande. Realizing that the progressive labor laws already on the books in Mexico could be used as a tool, he set out to bring strength to the workers. After years of contemplation, he understood the kind of organization that was needed. The Border Committee of Working Women in its depths and subtleties is the culmination of his life's effort.

I wanted to know more about Krueger's faith. I asked him if he saw the world in terms of good and evil.

"More in good than in evil," he said. "I think all people have dignity and worth—that's why I do what I do. My religion sustains me and gives direction to my life, because I see forgiving love as the heart of Christianity. But I'm not a fundamentalist. We've grown in our understanding of God. We need to be honest about the Bible and how it developed. We shouldn't, for instance, use the psalms, which ask for vengeance against others."

There was something uncomfortably saintlike about all this, the more so because Krueger's path is a difficult one, with no obvious destination. The *maquila* workers will never earn enough money or have easy lives. Neither will Krueger. He will die in obscurity and may never admit even to himself the effects he had in passing.

Brownsville, Texas, is the border's last city, an unloved place with a dirty brick downtown and a collection of *Ropa Usada* stores where mountains of used clothes are sold to Mexicans from across the Rio Grande. On its eastern edge, by the airport, stands a fenced compound that looks like a grammar school—a cluster of low buildings and verandas, people, some grass and trees. It is a refugee camp for Central Americans, run by the Catholic diocese and named Casa Oscar Romero after the Salvadoran archbishop who was assassinated in 1980. The camp accommodates two hundred people. Having swum the Rio Grande and evaded the Border Patrol, Central Americans can rest safely there for a week or two. The Border Patrol cruises by, but does not dare enter the grounds.

There are as many women as men. Some use the time to file for political asylum: while their requests are being processed, they cannot be deported. That is likely to change now, with no important effect. Most of the immigrants don't bother with procedure anyway, but simply eat and sleep before slipping away to the north. They hear about the camp from fellow travelers or from taxi drivers in Brownsville. Though the Border Patrol cannot find the immigrants in the bushes, apparently the taxi drivers can. Throughout the day I spent at the camp, taxis pulled up to the gate and discharged people, sometimes entire families. The drivers went the other way, too: a Honduran hired a cab to take him back to the river, to find his sisters whom he had left hiding. I do not know what became of them; the border is a dangerous place for immigrants, and hours later the Honduran had not returned.

I talked to a Guatemalan who had been to the United States five years before but had gotten drunk in Colorado and been arrested and deported. Back in Guatemala, he returned to his village, to his family of eight sisters and a brother. When his father was shot by the army, he decided to go north again to find another sister, who had married and was living in Miami. Each time, he spent three weeks getting through Mexico. Crossing the Rio Grande at Laredo, he was caught and thrown back four times. He avoided repatriation to Guatemala by claiming to be a Mexican. On the fifth attempt, here at Brownsville, he slipped by the Border Patrol. I asked him how he planned to get to Miami. He was not sure. I asked him how he would find his sister, and he admitted that he did not know her address or her married name. The camp was full of similar problems: a brother somewhere in Chicago, a cousin last heard of in Houston, obsolete addresses, disconnected telephones, people lost in the mass of human migration.

The white-haired nun in the camp office was a Spaniard and she was angry. She said, "You preach that here in the United States is paradise, and people believe you." A business jet, on a mission for the *maquilas,* screamed overhead. She said, "The big companies, they are miserable people with unlimited ambition. The suffering you see around you is the result of their greed. The border is a sore—the sickness is within us."

She was an ideologue, and she packaged the world as one. But she was right in the most important sense. The border is hardly some separate place.

Beyond the refugee camp, the land is mostly unused. Burdened with sewage and industrial runoff, the Rio Grande flows the last thirty miles across a dismal coastal flat. A bay to the north hems it in, making this lowest stretch of river unattractive to immigrants and smugglers. A paved road dwindles as it approaches the coast at a narrow, littered beach called Boca Chica. Where the pavement turns to sand, the state of Texas has planted a solid STOP sign, as if people would not otherwise know. Here the nation ends. After two thousand ambiguous miles, maybe the affirmation is necessary. I walked down the beach to where the Rio Grande emptied into the surf, and I sat in the sand watching the waters mix. Aware of the border stretching out behind me, I thought back to the ranch outside of Marfa and to the last time I had seen Ismael Zaragosa.

It was a decade ago. I had left the ranch and gone to New York for several months. When I returned, the crew cabin was empty and Ismael had disappeared, taking his wife Dora with him, leaving only the old bullet holes through the screens to mark his passage. The ranch seemed more desolate without him. After a few days I telephoned the rancher in Marfa to ask what had happened. He was a man named Bub. He called Ismael a worthless Mexican, and said he didn't know where he had gone and didn't care. He was annoyed that I asked and annoyed that I called. He had been drinking.

It was autumn, and the high-country nights had turned clear and cold. Sometimes I sat up late under the stars and out of habit listened to the Chihuahuan radio, the *Norteño* ballads and advertisements for Dr. Scholl's foot pads. When the migrants materialized, I fed them as usual and gave them a place to sleep in the sheds. One evening, after I passed them bread and sardines, several mentioned that they had heard about me from Ismael. They said he had moved back to the river and was living in Mexico. I asked why he had left the ranch. They exchanged glances, apparently surprised that I did not already know. They said he had been thrown by a horse and injured.

Eventually I took a pickup truck to the Rio Grande to find him. I started at the Candelaria store, where Nellie Howard said she had never heard of him. No one else there knew of him either. Mystified, I drove downriver to the next village on the Texas side, Ruidosa, where a grizzled old man cursed me and turned away without answering my question. I drove through the salt cedar down a rough track to the ford, and at the edge of the river spoke to young men in straw hats. They laughed at me and explained that Ismael Zaragosa was a fiction, the birth name of a dead American assumed by a Mexican from across the Rio Grande in the village called Verrancos. Someone had turned him in to U.S. Immigration and he had fled back to Mexico. They told me his real name, which I forget, and where he lived. They laughed again when I asked if a horse had thrown him.

But Ismael had indeed been hurt. I forded the river, and found him living in the desert, five miles outside of Verrancos. He and Dora had moved into a dirt-floor shack without electricity or water. I parked in the yard, and carried a bag of groceries through searing sunlight to the door. Dora greeted me solemnly and accepted the groceries without a fuss. She did not invite me in, but called to Ismael, who was sleeping on a corner cot in the dim interior. I looked away and noticed the drinking water stored in a rusted fifty-gallon drum, the latrine, and the litter in the yard. Ismael hobbled out of the shack, zipping up his pants. He looked pale. He explained that the horse had not thrown him, but had stopped suddenly, compressing and fracturing his spine against the saddle. A doctor in Ojinaga said someday he would feel less pain.

Dora was careful still to call him "Ismael" in my presence. She left us alone in the yard. Ismael told me she was afraid the river people would think I was a narcotics agent. The shack was on the main track from Ojinaga, and the traffickers were moving big loads. Ismael did not approve. He cursed to show me he had not changed. I smiled. We were both embarrassed by his poverty. His hair was long and ragged. He wore the tire-sole sandals of the poorest peasant, and his feet were dusty and cracked. I wondered if he had sold his boots. I did not bring up the question of his real identity or ask who had turned him in. We had little to say and he wanted me gone.